D1496216

*Opening day at the new Financial Trading Floor of
The Chicago Board of Trade 1982*

The First Woman
in the World
to Physically Trade
Thirty-Year Treasury Bonds
at the Chicago
Board of Trade

JOYCE, QUEEN OF' THE MOUNTAIN

Female Courage
and Hand-to-Hand
Combat in the World's
Largest Money Pit

BY **JOYCE SELANDER**

iUniverse, Inc.
Bloomington

Joyce, Queen of the Mountain
Female Courage and Hand-to-Hand Combat
in the World's Largest Money Pit

iUniverse books may be ordered through booksellers or by contacting:

iUniverse
1663 Liberty Drive
Bloomington, IN 47403
www.iuniverse.com
1-800-Authors (1-800-288-4677)

ISBN: 978-1-4620-4205-0 (sc)
ISBN: 978-1-4620-4207-4 (hc)
ISBN: 978-1-4620-4206-7 (e)

Library of Congress Control Number: 2011914244

Printed in the United States of America

iUniverse rev. date: 08/18/2011

With love to Mom and Dad for giving me strength and courage

Special thanks to my editor Cheryl Jefferson

This is a story about a fascinating time in our countries financial history and the changes that came because of it. It is also a story of a woman in a man's world and the huge success she achieves. Therefore, *Joyce, Queen of the Mountain* shows anyone with desire; brains and nerve can be successful. - Barry Lind, founder Lind Waldock

Joyce, Queen of the Mountain is awesome!!!! Thank-you for putting so many words of encouragement in this fabulous story. - Sylvia Long, President Longevous Capital, LLC

Joyce, Queen of the Mountain conveys a real sense of excitement and passion for the times, the people and the physical act of pit trading that we lived through. My first day on The Chicago Board of Trade floor in the late 1980's, the noise was deafening. Six or Seven hundred Bond traders and clerks yelling and shouting at the top of their lungs. There was a visceral thrill and adrenaline rush to the trading floor and the business in general that Joyce captures the spirit of in her book – Bryant Guy, Member CBOT

A must-read, high energy memoir by the first woman to trade financials in the pits at CBOT, a woman who achieved spectacular success in a man's world because she refused to become one of them and instead played by her own rules.
– Cheryl Jefferson, author of
  Use Your Anger: A Woman's
  Guide to Empowerment

"Joyce's story covers one of the most interesting periods in the futures industry. She provides an insiders view into the industry few others have revealed including insights into some of the industry's most interesting and colorful characters."
-Daniel P. Collins, Managing Editor, Futures Magazine Group

FOREWARD

From 1968 to the middle 90s, the futures pit and eventually the options pit was the place to be! Let' see …the markets opened about 9 a.m. and closed at 1 p.m., you didn't need a great education, seats were not real expensive, and if you couldn't afford to buy one, you could rent one; and if you only made $250,000 a year you were nobody. Another benefit if you were young was that a lot of pretty women came down to the Exchange to find a husband, but in any event your afternoons were free.

It was all men, we smoked in the pit, oh and by the way, U.S. tax rules allowed you to roll your profits into the next year so effectively, you didn't have to pay any taxes. I shouldn't forget that if you were a good guy and you were liked, you could go broke at least three times before people wouldn't lend you money for a new start. Sounds like a great situation. It was.

There was a lot to learn. Walking into the pit for the first time was like being in a box seat at a major league ball game right by the dugout, yelling at the pitcher about how bad he was and suddenly, the manager comes out and says, "You think he's so bad, you pinch hit for the next batter." You're facing Randy Johnson and 240,000 people in the stands. I never had that experience (I was never picked higher than 5th in any choose up game) but I can compare that experience to the first time I was in the pit with all these experts. The only success I had that day was that I didn't wet my pants.

Don't get me wrong, most people who tried trading futures didn't make a quarter of a million dollars a year, they actually failed. Far more failed than had even moderate success. It takes a lot to be a good trader, let alone a good pit trader. You have to have an ego just to walk into the pit but you can never let your ego get in the way. Stubbornness has destroyed more wannabe's than anything else. You have to be smart, you have to be mentally strong, you have to admit when you are wrong, you have to be quick, you have to have great nerve, you have to learn from your mistakes, you have to know when to have patience, you have to develop a method that works for you and you have to be physical.

Did I tell you it was all men; we smoked in the pit, that the first time in the pit was like facing Randy Johnson. Well, let's see …I got better at facing Randy Johnson every day and after months, he retired. Eventually, they banned smoking in the pit, then on the floor, and eventually in the building. Then in 1969, the government that let us postpone our taxes told us we had to let women in the pit and actually allow them to trade. For women to trade in the pit had to be a lot tougher than me facing Randy Johnson, and for a woman to develop the mental strength to take on the markets as well standing up to our male part of the world required some very special qualities. Most women weren't even in business those days.

You are about to read about that special kind of woman! I have known Joyce Selander for over forty years, from when she was a very pretty, very smart, eager twenty-five year old clerk to when she was one of the most successful women in the futures industry. I think you will find her experience most interesting, very entertaining, and it has a good chance of making you a stronger person.

Ex-Young Turk
Barry Lind
Founder, Lind Waldock

THE PREFACE

Dear Reader,

Have you ever been in the pits - literally? I have, and now I want to take you there. My name is Joyce Selander and I was the first woman to physically trade financial futures in the pits at the Chicago Board of Trade. At barely 5'5", 110 pounds dripping wet, I went into physical, hand-to-hand financial combat everyday for thirteen years. Standing - or trying to stand - toe-to-toe with five hundred shouting, sweating, testosterone hyped male traders (and 1500 frantic clerks!) all driven by ambition, need, greed, love, and sometimes, desperation. Every one of them was trying to reach the top of the financial mountain, just like me.

Some days that mountaintop was far away. I would leave the floor mentally bruised, physically black and blue, and fighting tears. Even when I exited the building I was always in the pits - down on the days I lost thousands, up on the days when the market was up along with my amazing life. Through my work I met diplomats and US presidents; dated secret service agents; saw murder, mayhem, a personal plot to overthrow the Taliban, and everything in between including remarkable kindness and grace under pressure.

So join me on this incredible adventure which started when smoking was permitted in the pits but women were not. And the next time you think you can't take it anymore, that you'll never make it, I'm here to tell you, you will. Your feminine dignity and power will triumph. You can conquer and become queen of your mountain, just like me.

Regards,
Joyce Selander

CONTENTS

Chapter One

FIRST DAY AT SCHOOL

I was four-and-a-half years old when my mother took me to my first day of kindergarten at Trumbull Elementary. It was in Andersonville, a middle-class Swedish neighborhood on Chicago's north side. Hand-in-hand we walked into the classroom where my young eyes were surprised by the large number of crying children and their consoling mothers. "Who," I asked my mom, "are all these whiny kids?"

Looking tenderly at me she explained that these children were frightened because it was their first day of school and they would soon be left alone. Should she stay with me awhile? Mom clasped my hand tighter. No! I said immediately. I was fine on my own, then I proceeded to explore the classroom.

I found a newly filled sandbox with a giant mound of sand. Jumping on the pile, I screamed at the top of my lungs "I am Joyce, Queen of the Mountain!" But Johnny, the local bully, charged up the side shouting "No, I am the mountain King!" Like a boxer, I punched his chest with a closed fist and sent him flying. *Anybody else?* I thought, scanning the startled kindergarteners. No. Triumphant, I proclaimed again "I am Joyce, Queen of the Mountain!'

Little did I know then how hard it would be to stay on top. You see, on that day, there were no other challengers, but there have been plenty since I became the first woman to trade financial futures in the pits at the Chicago Board of Trade. Thirty year Treasury Bonds to be exact, that's actual U.S. government bonds, notes and t-bills, the biggest market in the world where numbers are king.

Now numbers, their adding and subtracting, multiplying and dividing have always come easy to me. A natural gift. I remember my kindergarten teacher asking, "Who can count to ten? Who can count above ten?" My right hand shot up and she called on me saying "Joyce, count for us." 12345678910 Jack Queen King Ace I answered proudly. My mother would have beamed and my father would have blushed. You see, I started playing family poker when I was four. I proved a fast learner and by age six, I could shuffle and set up a full house or straight on the bottom of the deck.

Maybe I knew something about numbers because my mother had graduated from college (rare in those days, the 1930s) and taken a job at a bank. When I turned fifteen she got me a part-time job working there on Saturdays. It was a neighborhood bank and by the time I was sixteen, the savings manager had taught me to balance her department. By the time I was 17, I knew how to balance the entire bank. Banking became my livelihood while I was attending college. I started working at a downtown Chicago bank as a teller and margin clerk. That meant I was in charge of computing margins on loans secured by marketable collateral such as stocks and bonds. One day, I received a call from a headhunter who asked me if I could calculate margins on commodities. I told her sure, why not. You take the daily value and fluctuation then use a percentage to figure out how much money the customer needs to maintain his position. On hearing my answer, the headhunter arranged an interview for me the very next week.

That interview turned out to be with Maurie Schneider, owner and president of M-S Commodities. His father, 80 year old Sol Schneider, was one of the founders of the Chicago Mercantile Exchange. Of course, Maurie hired me on the spot.

Two days after I started working at M-S, I strolled into Maurie's office and informed him that one of his branch offices was illegally moving funds. "What!" Maurie stared at me as I explained that someone was taking money from account A and moving it to account B. "That can't be," Maurie protested. His company had just been audited the week before I joined them. Immediately, he picked up the phone, called his auditors and said, "You'd better get over here immediately. I have a mini-skirted girl with a beehive telling me you guys screwed up."

The very next day Maurie sent me, mini-skirt, beehive and all, down to the trading floor of the Chicago Mercantile Exchange to see exactly what the traders at his M–S trading desk were doing. The moment I stepped onto that floor I knew this was it, what I wanted to do with the rest of my life. When the market closed and everyone left, I walked to the top of the trading pit and took it all in. I came, I saw, and now I wanted to conquer. I am *Joyce,* I said softly to myself, *Queen of the Mountain.*

Chapter Two

THE CHICAGO MERCANTILE EXCHANGE - (CME)

It was 1968 and the Chicago Mercantile Exchange (CME) was re-inventing itself. There were 500 members including three women - Kathy White, who ran a small desk for one of the large floor brokers; a second woman who had a membership but because of exchange rules was not allowed into the pit where the actual, physical trading takes place; and me.A lot of people would be intimidated by such a high pressure environment with a 500 to 3 ratio but those were My Kind of Odds. Besides, it was easy to make friends, lots of friends, all men.

I made many of these friends in a small, members only coffee shop where the big traders played cards when the markets were slow. Maurie would take me there and introduce me, which gave me the chance to meet everyone. It was on these caffeine excursions that I met the two geniuses of the Commodity Industy. One was the visionary Leo Melamed, CME Chairman, then a young man with a grand plan for the future. The other was twenty-eight year old Barry Lind, CME's equally brilliant Director and the founder of Lind Waldock and Company which eventually became the largest commodity retail brokerage house on the planet. This dynamic duo, together with other CME members, became known as the Young Turks. Together, they shook the Commodities Industry with the massive, forward thinking changes that transformed CME into the enormous, powerhouse it is today - a far cry from where the exchange originated.

★   ★   ★

Our origins were as The Chicago Butter and Egg Exchange which was organized back in 1898. By 1919, we had become the Chicago Mercantile Exchange and eventually, began trading frozen pork bellies (1961), and live cattle, (1964).

By the time I arrived in 1968, there were only three active, open out cry trading pits. The pits were large circles, twenty-five to thirty feet in diameter and four feet deep, with one wooden step up and two or three steps down. Each held forty to fifty traders. The men would stand in these pits yelling bids and offers on prices of various commodity products including frozen pork bellies, live cattle, and live hogs. In addition, there were about a hundred old fashioned, high-backed trading desks. The wooden backs were hung with dozens of phones easily accessed by the standing traders. Likewise, the desktops were high so you could write orders while standing up, then quickly hand them to a runner who took them to the pit broker. Traders originally wrote these orders under dimly lit chandeliers. Eventually, the ceiling was lowered and the chandeliers were replaced with brighter, modern lighting that allowed us to more clearly see the mechanical boards on the walls and the chalkboards positioned beneath them. But even with this upgrade, the place was dark, dingy, and "Noisy" can't begin to describe it. So why was it the only place in the whole, wide world I wanted to be? Maybe it was the daily action - and I'm not just talking about the five hundred men.

The frantic, organized, incredibly exciting chaos went like this. Eggs were traded on the south wall chalkboards. A member would give the quantity plus the bid or sale price to a CME employee who would grab chalk, then write the information on the big boards so all the traders could see the new order and the change of price that had occurred, setting off a wave of activity.

Across the room, there would be an even bigger wave with the Pork Bellies Futures and the Live Cattle Futures. Back then, Pork Bellies Futures were the largest actively traded commodity with Live Cattle Futures a close second. In August of 1968, the total volume of frozen pork bellies was 108,791 contracts. One year later, that volume surged to 160,632 contracts. Likewise, in August of 1968, live cattle total volume was 16,521 contracts. By August, 1969, that number skyrocketed to 125,519 contracts. Eventually, cattle futures surpassed pork bellies in volume and open interest. The bottom line was this. During my first year at the M-S Commodities trading desk, I saw cattle volume expand nine times its size and pork bellies volume go up 50,000 contracts. And I was part of it.

My morning always began with checking my margin calls and debits, and talking with my direct boss, Priscilla. Then I'd quickly head to the trading pit for the opening of the market. When the market closed I'd dash back upstairs to my office to complete any margin calls I hadn't finished. After a few days, I was promoted to floor manager, responsible for the trading desk and instructing the clerks. Priscilla would come down to the floor every few hours to pick up filled orders and make sure everything was running smoothly. The bottom line was this - my career was happening and it was happening so fast I couldn't believe it. To keep up, I had to study like mad. I learned all the Rules and Regulations of the CME and the CFTC, the Commodity Futures Trading Commission which was orginally called the Commodity Exchange Act (CEA). Soon I became a walking encyclopedia, but all this knowledge didn't prepare me for the unusual, highly necessary responsibility Maurie now assigned me, to physically remove his eighty year old father, Sol, from the pork belly or hog pit if the market went wild, entering into fast or limit conditions. But this was easier said than done.

Every time I entered the trading pit to take Maurie's Dad out of harm's way, I would be fined because it was still against CME regulations for a woman to enter the pit. In addition, a lot of older traders like Sol were not happy with my presence in the trading arena. Sol would hand me a comb and tell me to go comb my hair, my stylish beehive! Every time, I would end up taking the comb and Sol back to the trading desk. (I also kept my beehive intact!)

Finally, the President of the Exchange, Everette B. Harris, called me into his office. He chastised me for breaking the rules and for aggravating the members. I gently sassed him back, informing him of my situation and pointing out that the rules had to change if CME planned to keep up with the times. Of course, I knew all these men wanted to "Keep up" so it was no surprise when they took my advice and hired women to work on the trading floor and to track trades on the chalk boards. At long last, I wasn't the lone mini-skirted girl, but to my chagrin, the CME now made women wear slacks or skirts at the knee. Damn! Oh well, it was good to have female company. - especially with the explosion that was about to occur.

The first rumble was in 1972 when currencies opened. By 1977, U.S. Bonds were trading at the Chicago Board of Trade; followed by Eurodollars in 1981; and S&P 500 Futures in 1982. A whole new world called derivatives was born and technology multiplied the opportunity. With the opening of CME's Globex electronic trading (1992) we could now trade across the globe every hour of the day. That meant the CME not only had to move to a bigger floor, we had to think bigger, much bigger, and we did.

On July 9, 2007, the Chicago Mercantile Exchange officially merged with the Chicago Board of Trade and became the CME Group. But we didn't stop there. Approximately one year later (8/22/08), CME Group acquired the New York Mercantile Exchange, surpassing all challengers to become the largest Commodity Exchange in the world. Today, CME Group trades more than three hundred and fifty different commodities, derivatives, and option contracts simultaneously twenty-four hours a day, six days a week, which just goes to show what a handful of brilliant, determined men, and I'd like to think, one mini-skirted girl can accomplish.

Chapter Three

CHICAGO, 1968

When most people think of Chicago, 1968, they think of the Democratic National Convention, the riots, the hippies, and the free love. I think of one Dennis Patrick Shaw who I met at the end of the convention. He was the Lead Advance Secret Service Agent in charge of the eventual winner of the presidential race, Richard Nixon. Now Denny was young, tall, and hot, a James Bond type with dark brown hair and darker brown eyes. He stood 6'3" and was 220 magnificent pounds of rippling muscle. I started dating Denny and suddenly found myself commuting to New York, Washington, and Key Biscayne, and of course, he got to the Windy City regularly.

One spring night in 1969, Denny called and said President Nixon was flying into Chicago. Would I pick him up - Denny, not the President, at the airport? You bet. In fact, I couldn't get there fast enough so it's a mystery why I was running so late. Frantic, I drove up to the main gate for the military side of O'Hare International Airport. Security quickly waved me through because Denny had put my name on the list. But I was still late so I punched it, doing forty miles per hour in the parking lot. Suddenly an MP - a military police officer - pulled me over. He swaggered to my car barking "Where you going ma'am?" Ma'am!?!! If you want to see my blood boil, just call my svelte self "Ma'am" especially if you're coming at me with an open ticket book.

★   ★   ★

Sweetly, (my ass!) I informed him that I was going to meet Richard Nixon, the President of the United States. The MP demanded my drivers license, then called security to see if I was really on the list. When he discovered that I was on the list, he sulkily returned my license, warning me to drive slow and head straight down the road. Sure I would. As soon as he turned away I rammed my little Volkswagen into gear and floored it. I was doing forty across this wide road when I heard a sound. A very loud, very scary sound. Oh cripes! Over my shoulder Air Force One was bearing down and dropping fast. Holy shit! I put the pedal to the medal, careened off the runway and parked my car. Suddenly, my Volkswagen was surrounded by Secret Service Agents about to draw their guns. There was only one thing to do.

I opened the car door and slowly slid out, legs out first. Make that boots first because I was wearing impossibly tight, black patent leather knee high boots with three inch heels. They were boots made for walking and that's just what I would do. Slowly, I stepped forward so the men could get a good look at my favorite Chanel black and white houndstooth suit with the jacket tailored to accent my micro-mini skirt and matching small rimmed jockey hat. One of the agents grinned. "Hi Joyce, he said, "The president's plane has landed." And so had I.

As everyone deplaned and piled into waiting limousines, Denny walked over and put his gorgeous face close to mine. *"Nice job,"* he says. "We were coming in for the landing and over the Secret Service radio I hear alert, blue Volkswagen crossing the runway. The pilots started to question if they should abort the landing and then over the radio we hear "It's O.K., it's Shaw's girlfriend, Joyce." Denny rolled his eyes. "I will never live this down."

I'll make it up to you! I gave Shaw a big kiss to show I always kept my promises. He hopped into my car and we drove downtown to the Blackstone Hotel where we took the elevator upstairs to Secret Service headquarters. As we entered the room, an agent walked up and tapped Denny on the back.

"Here's the photo of the bomb we defused at O'Hare," he said, showing Denny the picture. "It was big enough to blow up one-third of the airport." I say a little prayer of thanks that Denny and the other agents protecting the President are so good at what they do.

On Mr. Nixon's next visit to Chicago, Denny asked me to come to the lobby of the Blackstone Hotel. When I arrived, the place was totally empty. I was standing alone, wondering what was going on when the President, Mrs. Nixon, and Denny walked in. As the two men stopped to chat with the hotel manager, Mrs. Nixon walked along the red velvet, roped off area toward me. She stopped for a moment, waiting for her husband and Denny. "Good afternoon, Mrs. Nixon," I said.

"Hi Joyce, nice to see you," Pat Nixon smiled.

I just about fell over. How did she know my name?

Then President Nixon saw the two of us standing together - her without visible protection. Walking up he lightly clasped Mrs. Nixon's arm, moving her close to him and away from me. He was being very cautious but she said "Richard, you know Denny Shaw's girlfriend, Joyce."

Relieved, the President smiled. "Nice to see you," he said. Then they walked away.

As I looked after them I couldn't believe the President of the United States had spoken to me and the First Lady had called me by name, Joyce. And even though Mr. Nixon's term ended under a dark cloud, at that moment there were no clouds over my mountain, in fact, I felt like I had touched the stars.

Chapter Four

THE INTERNATIONAL MONETARY MARKET

If CME had had a book club in 1971, the reading material of choice would've been *The Need for Futures Markets in Currencies,* by Dr. Milton Friedman, a monetary concerns specialist and eventual Nobel Prize winner in economics who, at the time, was beginning to make a name for himself as the expert in international currency relationships. Over at the Chicago Mercantile Exchange, Leo Melamed, CME Chairman, and Everette Harris, CME President, needed no convincing. Behind closed doors, they were working on the very thing Friedman proposed. In fact, Leo had encouraged Friedman to write about a startup marketplace for currency trading as futures.

But in August of '71, the future got a shock when President Nixon suddenly announced he would stop exchanging gold for dollars. Not only that, he raised the price of bullion from $35 an ounce to $38 an ounce. It was the first change in the official price of gold in thirty-seven years and the move shook the commodity industry to its core. Average Americans reeled from the aftershocks, too. The dollar's devaluation meant we would pay more for foreign cars, imported goods, and face Stagflation in the late 1970's.

But in May of 72, this was barely a blip on the radar. CME had just opened the International Monetary Market (IMM) Futures contracts -- the world's first and only futures market with a centralized, flexible price. Now there had always been a cash market on foreign currencies at different banks in different countries, but CME was the first to centralize the trade in one major area. This meant that every bank and everybody around the globe could trade and hedge. Among those bodies were 1000 new IMM members in addition to the 500 existing CME members. With all these players, market volume skyrocketed, tripling in just one year. I was on an equally good trajectory. Just before IMM trading officially opened, I got a phone call from Leo Melamed who said he had a job for me. He'd been talking to one of the new market's originators, Dr. Henry Jarecki. Dr. Jarecki was starting a floor operation and Leo had recommended me for Floor Manager.

WOW! A chance to work with Dr. Jarecki! It didn't get any better than this (happily, I would say that several more times in my career). I was in, but little did I know I was going to work for GOLDFINGER, at least, that's what many of the traders called him. A stocky, heavy-set man with a blotchy complexion, Dr. Jarecki of Mocatta a fifth generation gold bullion distributor/dealer was of average height with dark hair and bespectacled eyes. He'd graduated from the University of Heidelberg Medical School and later owned an island in the British Virgin chain with species of fish, birds, and flowers that don't exist anywhere else on earth. If you believed the rumors, he was also the proud owner of land-to-air missiles he'd purchased from the Russians, which might explain his soft, appealing manner and the fact that he never needed to raise his voice.

What he did need was the ability to hedge currencies, something essential to the international gold bullion trade and to global foreign exchange. Dr. Jarecki's business, Mocatta Metals, was the largest gold and silver trading company on the planet. He also owned the Brody White Commodity House. Unfortunately, my job there was short-lived because he decided not to establish his own clearing house (a very costly proposition) at this time. Instead, Dr. Jarecki took the more popular, economical option of paying a member fee and going through someone else's floor desk.

Even so, I learned a lot about gold, silver and currency trading, and even more about the Art of Arbitrage. Arbitrage is the simultaneous trading of similar commodities in different markets across the world. It was complex and I was learning from one of the best, a bright, powerful man who I liked and enjoyed being around. Dr. Jarecki was also one of the first traders to integrate computer systems into trading programs. What a privilege to be part of that evolution. No wonder I loved running into him on the floor of the Chicago Board of Trade. He was GOLDFINGER, the man with the golden touch. This applied to many of his staff, too.

I worked with that staff daily since I set up and ran the IMM floor operation for Jarecki's companies, taking currency orders from his brokers by phone and reporting the fills back to his New York and London offices. The Mocatta Metals brokers were great and they taught me the minutiae and nuances of gold and currencies. Once, Dr. Jarecki sent a floor broker from the London Metals Exchange (the LME) to Chicago to work with me. This was a big, husky British guy married to a bunny who worked at the newly opened Playboy Club in London. The Brit traded currencies for himself, our brokers, clients, and for the company. Like most traders, he added good liquidity by making two-sided markets, that is, a standing bid and an offer. This strategy kept the gap between the bid and the offer spread as close as possible which ultimately, brought in new business. That business was important. And fascinating.

The Trading Floor was made up of small, individual pits for each currency. The first tradable contracts were in the British pound, Canadian dollar, German mark, Japanese yen, Mexican peso, Swiss franc and Italian lira (although the lira didn't trade very long). It was easy to move from one area to another to spread the British pound against Swiss francs, German marks, or Japanese yen. Being able to hedge a gold or grain sale in the currency used for its purchase was critical. You see, before the IMM markets opened, we couldn't lock in a foreign currency price against the dollar. In other words, there was no way to hedge or protect the purchase or sale of goods for a specific amount, versus fluctuations in a foreign currency. If a company had sold grains or gold and the foreign currency went down in value, that company lost money on the price of its transactions. This could offset the appreciation of the company's gold or grain position.

The opening of the IMM currency markets changed all that. Companies now had the ability to lock in the price of their transactions in the futures market. This is why currency pits are critical to world trade and many import/export businesses. It's also why the birth of the IMM was a cause for celebration and boy, did Dr. Jarecki know how to celebrate.

He had GREAT parties. I wasn't allowed to attend many and when I did, well, I ain't tellin'. But I did hear about some totally wild and notorious antics. Yes, there was the standard array of drunken men dancing on the tables with WILD WOMEN, but my own anthropological studies went deeper. From my many years of experience, I knew that different types of people traded different types of commodities. My Iowa farmers were nice, clean-cut All-American boys, well-mannered, sweet who liked to have fun (and they did too!). Gold and Silver traders were a different breed, vintage BAD BOYS, crazy risk-takers who went for the big Kahuna. Case in point.

The day after one of these parties, a guy who'd attended came down on the floor. He looked like a cowboy. He wore cowboy boots and a cowboy hat and was bow legged with curly hair that was a little too long. He resembled Custer after the last stand, only nastier and dirtier. In a voice loud enough for me to hear, "Custer" was telling the traders about an episode earlier that day. He'd gone to his bank vault and removed all his gold and silver. In a private room, he carefully stacked all his silver bricks on the table and put the gold bars atop the silver ones. Then he brought in a tall blonde woman with magnificent breasts and long legs to see his gold. He removed all her clothes and screwed her on top of the precious metal while singing "Goldfinger," the theme from the James Bond movie of the same name. I just hope he had a good voice because he sure didn't have looks, manners, or taste to compensate. It gave new meaning to the phrase "All that glitters..."

Speaking of which, a glittering array of celebrities, politicians, and foreign diplomats came to check out our new market. Visitors were on the trading floor all day long and opening day was bonkers. Besides the Chicago and New York press, there were foreign correspondents photographing everyone and everything in sight. Because everybody in the pit was required to wear a jacket and badge and we were short on the former, I gave mine to Mickey Carol Norton, the first woman member /trader of the IMM. But I was still within camera range, and

I heard later that a foreign paper published a gigantic picture of me screaming and signaling a trade -- except that I was wearing a pink silk turtleneck. A pink silk turtleneck that aluminized under the flashbulb light so you could see right through it. I appeared to be trading in just a lacy French bra. The exchange was upset, but who knows, maybe it was good for foreign relations. Or at least a good laugh.

Now, Mickey Carol Norton laughed a lot. A very petite blonde woman with a sense of humor and a nice shape, she could be feisty and that served her well. Very well as she became one of the owners of the six-time world champion Chicago Bulls professional basketball team and outlasted most of the men who started with her in the IMM. Like me, she is still a member today. How did we do it? How do we continue to do it? Persistence. We stand toe-to-toe with the men and never back down. We never break stride either. Did I say stride? I really mean strut. We strut our professional stuff and smile like we know it all. And you know what? Sometimes we do.

1973 Opening day of the International Monetary Market (IMM) at the Chicago Mercantile Exchange

Chapter Five

THE CHICAGO BOARD OF TRADE

It was 1972. I was still calling the CME home when suddenly the opportunity arose to move to larger house, a much larger house, The Chicago Board of Trade (CBOT). With 1407 members, and a trading floor double the CME's size, CBOT was (and is) the largest Grain Exchange in the world. I moved there to work for Conti-Commodities, the new customer division of Continental Grain. A privately held organization, Continental Grain was the second largest grain company on earth with - as its name suggests - offices on almost every continent.

And CBOT's early members probably thought they could see those continents through their office windows since they were working in what was then the tallest building in Chicago (surpassed by the Richard J. Daley Center in 1965). Originally opened for business on April 3, 1848, then forced to move in 1871, when the Great Chicago Fire destroyed its first home, CBOT was rebuilt at LaSalle and Jackson streets in May, 1885. The current building, now the primary trading place for CBOT and the CME, opened its doors and its 19,000 square foot trading floor in 1930. And what a floor and doors they are.

Registered as both a Chicago and a National Historic Landmark, the Chicago Board of Trade building is one of the finest surviving examples of Art Deco architecture anywhere in the world. With massive stone carvings and sculptures, the building's facade features a thirteen foot clock looking down on LaSalle Street. On both sides of the dial are huge, hooded figures, one a mysterious Egyptian holding grain, the other, a Native American holding corn. At the very top of the building stands a three story, Art Deco statue of Ceres, the goddess of grains. She was so big, I could actually see her from my penthouse studio home on Lake Shore Drive. I liked to think she was watching out for me -- not only me -- but everyone who entered the building.

The entryway is so beautiful, you could actually strain your neck looking up at the three-story lobby. The first thing you see are stunning brass owls above each doorway. Symbolically, the owls protect the grain we trade by chasing away birds and killing mice that might eat the harvest. The fruit of that harvest is depicted everywhere including the second floor brass railings and carved inserts over the doors that look like bundles of wheat. The brass is accented by beige marble floors and black and white marble walls. On the second and third floors, the walls are tan marble and they ripple upward like clouds. The elevators that take you up into these marble-y clouds have black doors with tall, brass art deco stalks of wheat, flowering on top in a triangular pattern. Stunning in a different but equally impressive way, is the twenty-three story expansion completed in 1982, which gave CBOT an additional, 32,000 square foot, four story trading floor.

Amazing as all these structural features are, I think the most important architectural gem in the whole building was (and is!) the entrance to the Sign of the Trader Bar and Restaurant. Packed by 1:30 in the afternoon until closing time at 8:00 pm. The Chicago Tribune Magazine said the Sign poured more liquor than any other bar in the city. That's saying a lot since Chicago is a hard drinking town and the Sign is only open Monday through Friday.

The Sign's reputation, along with the building's beautiful interior and exterior, might explain why so many movies are filmed here and next door at the old Continental Bank Building, now the Bank of America. The Dark Knight was one of these. As I was leaving one afternoon with our company intern, Petr Hudec, of the Czech Republic, we ran into a man wearing everyday clothes and odd white makeup on his bumpy looking face. I'm standing right next to him, thinking who is this guy when suddenly he looks at me, winks, then smiles. It was HEATH LEDGER! talking to his director. Even in partial Joker makeup (no lips yet) he made my heart beat faster. In fact, my heart often beat faster at the corner Jackson and LaSalle and it wasn't just the taxis using pedestrians for target practice! At that intersection, I've met U.S. presidents and foreign dignitaries; politicians, dancers, actors, and Nobel Prize winners; football, baseball and hockey players; and a list of prominent people too long to mention. Several of them became friends including Ron Young, the president of Conti-Commodities, my employer.

In addition to Ron, I worked with many large grain traders who are still friends today. They helped lure me into the trading business including Rick "The Rocket" Barnes and Kenny Mitchell. Always willing to buy or sell, Kenny was the best scalper in the soybean pit. Then there was Chuck Wafer, the best looking man on the CBOT floor, known for his large soybean positions. Soybeans and grain had become my world and it was fascinating, so fascinating that after three years with Conti, I moved to Cargill Inc., the words largest, privately held grain company. I was in its customer division called Cargill Investors Services (CIS).

One night after work and drinks at our local spot, The Sign of the Trader, we decided to order pizza and play cards at my place. Everyone loved my little penthouse in the sky. At night, looking out the windows, the whole city was lit up and sparkling, plus, we were high enough up that it was hard for anyone to see in when the guys decided to play strip poker. I wasn't worried because my palms were hot and itching, an old gypsy sign that you're going to make a lot of money. Sure enough, I just kept winning. As the game progressed, I finally lost one hand and had to take something off so I removed my right false eyelash. We argued whether removing an eyelash was legal, but I won the argument (naturally!) and eventually I took off the left one when I lost another hand.

But the guy who lost it all was Rick Barnes and he was hilarious. Down to his jockey shorts, he ducked into my bathroom, took a sheet out of my clothes hamper, and wrapped himself up like a Roman god. Sure enough, he lost the next hand so Rick took off his shorts but hung onto that sheet for dear life. We laughed so hard and loudly the woman downstairs called the doorman to complain. Since it was only 8:30 PM, I hoped he would tell her to turn up her television or close a few doors but he didn't. Finally, our pizza arrived and we continued eating, drinking, and laughing at Rick's sheet. Maybe my neighbor should have joined us because she clearly needed more fun in her life!

And Rick Barnes was fun with a capital "F." A blonde-haired, blue-eyed, California boy, Rick was stocky, 5'10", and always smiling through the ups and downs of trading. At first there were a lot of these, he'd make a million, lose a million, make three million, lose three million. Finally, Rich Dennis of C&D Commodities talked Rick into leaving the floor and coming upstairs to trade with him. It proved to be a good decision. Rick made 30 million dollars in soybeans in one year and never looked back. He just kept making money and loads of it. According to Chuck Wafer, Rick owns a horse farm in Ireland and a castle in Majorca, Spain where he lives today.

Chuck didn't do so badly himself. The manager of the Conti-Commodities office in Denver, I helped talk Chuck into moving to Chicago to trade grains on his own. He traded large limit positions and managed to make a lot of money. At six feet four inches tall and husky, he resembled a football player or the late movie star Christopher Reeve who portrayed Superman. Looking at Chuck was one of my job perks. So was enjoying the company of the great guys with whom I worked.

Since my place was right in the heart of Rush Street (Chicago's legendary bar district) the guys would always end up there, usually half, if not totally in the bag. Vince Schreiber, a cattle trader, and Pat Boyle, a wheat trader, lived in the western suburbs - a long drive from downtown Chicago. Late one night, they'd really tied one on and the two of 'em fell into my place without warning. Of course, I didn't mind (it was better to have them here than on the road driving!) They flipped a coin to see who would get the floor and who would get the couch but they were both so drunk they lost the coin! I finally threw two pillows on the carpet and both men bunked there.

Now a guy who rarely lost a coin of any denomination was Billy O'Connor. I first met Billy in 1968, on the CME floor. He'd started at CBOT, but business was slow so he came over to the CME for awhile to fill orders for Merrill Lynch. Billy had purchased his CME membership for $18,000 and later, in 1969, talked his brother, Eddie, into buying one, too. Unfortunately, Eddie paid the all-time high of $28,000 but maybe it wasn't such a bad deal considering that today, those memberships are worth eight to ten million dollars each. Why didn't I buy one then? I'm still kicking myself over that. Maybe I was too dazzled by Billy to think straight. He was your typical, good-looking, thirty something Irishman sporting a full head of beautiful white hair with silver highlights, accented by brilliant blue eyes that lit up when I entered the room. Those eyes lit up even more when Billy and I left the CME. He was returning to CBOT just as I started working there. We had a lifelong friendship that went on until he died and I still miss him. Now occasionally, we would have cocktails at Butch McGuire's, a legendary Chicago watering hole, where a few mutual friends would join us. We often talked about O'Connor and Company, Billy and Eddie's CBOT grain business.

During those talks, I used to kid Billy that everything he touched turned green. In fact, green was the only color he could see. Billy was colorblind and if his wife didn't put out his socks for him he would show up wearing one that was navy and one that was black. But maybe Billy's green vision was a blessing in disguise because eventually he and Eddie became the wealthiest, most well known traders at the CBOT. They would also open up one of the first, large proprietary trading companies and eventually, I would become one of their biggest brokers in the stock index pit.

As one of Billy and Eddie's friends and as one of the few women at the exchange, I was invited to the O'Connor & Company St. Patrick's Day Party. This annual holiday celebration was legendary and huge. For many years it was the biggest event at the exchange with more than a thousand people attending. All our cocktailing buddies from the Merc Vince, Harvey, Cadillac Jack and others would come over to play and I could hardly wait for the big day.

Finally, March 17 arrived. I was ready for the party and all the fun and I was dressed for the occasion in a knockout dark green wrap dress with shamrock shaped white leaves, a wide wrapped belt at the waist, and tiny white buttons which I had unbuttoned a little on the LOOOOOW side. The finishing touch was a green headband with two glittering shamrocks sticking up and bobbing back and forth. I looked good, I felt good, and I was ready to party when the phone rang. It was the president of Cargill asking me to come to his office to meet some people from the company's main branch.

With my shamrocks shaking and my boobs bouncing, I entered the room where two men were waiting to talk to me. The younger man turned to the older one with this look that said, "Who is this weirdo?" Then they explained that they had just finished designing a whole new computer system incorporating balance sheets, customer statements, and so forth. The pair had marching orders to get my approval. You see, Cargill had recently purchased the largest cattle feed operation in the country and had begun hedging live cattle and hogs. They came to me because I was the only person in the company who had experience in trading and balancing CME commodities. Right there in my shamrocks, I started checking out the new system page by page, but quickly handed the documents back to them. "It's all very nice," I smiled sweetly, "But you're missing two digits on all the cattle, hog and pork belly prices. For your information, live stock trade in 2 1/2 points per tick."

They looked at me like I'd turned into some kind of demented lady leprechaun. Patiently, I explained that the price movements were 60 cents to 62 1/2, 65 to 67 1/2 to 70 cents. In other words, it moved in increments of two and a half cents and they had neglected to calculate the half cent - a small amount but a BIG DEAL. Why? The cattle contract was 40,000 pounds times 2 1/2 cents which equaled ten dollars a tick, not eight. If they didn't fix this, their office would consistently be on the outs with my figures in small amounts of 30 and 50 dollars which would really add up fast. The men rolled their eyes, then the younger one said to his boss, "Now we know why the main branch told us to check with Joyce." They promised to redo the entire system to get those two critical digits in. Smiling I said goodbye and headed off to the best St. Paddy's party ever.

About a week later, I received a call from Cargill headquarters in Minnesota. I thought it might be about the computer system, but it was something far more entertaining. The five Cargill and McMillan grandsons were coming to town. All college age and ready to take their places in the family dynasty, they wanted to tour the CME floor. Well any reason to visit the CME and see all my old buddies was greatly appreciated by me so we met at the Cargill office in the CBOT building and made the short walk over.

It was the perfect time to visit because the CME floor was busy and there was a lot going on. My guests were quite surprised at the similarities between the Merc and the CBOT. The Merc was (and is) smaller but more modern with up-to-date electronic boards. We walked through and I showed them the cattle, hog, and pork bellies pits. Like any good tour guide, I pointed out that the hand signals, bid and offer terminology differed slightly for each exchange. I also made some introductions since my buddies hadn't seen me in awhile and everyone was coming over to say hello. As the boys and I reached the most important live cattle pit, the trading went WILD. Then my visitors got more than they bargained for. My friends, Harvey Paffenroth and Vince Schreiber started yelling at the top of their lungs "CHOICE JOYCE!" and they weren't talking about my cattle expertise.

The Cargill kids thought this was so hysterical they practically busted a gut laughing. They were also surprised at how many people I knew. All the while, the cattle pit continued to trade heavily and noisily, keeping my guests thoroughly entertained. While I was explaining the activity, several of the traders' clerks kept running over and handing me trading cards with cute little messages written on them. They were funny, too, because the clerks acted like the notes were orders pertaining to business. In reality, they were invitations to lunch, drinks, or dessert of a more personal nature and everybody (except my visitors) knew what was going on. You see, trading cards have the member's acronym on the top so everybody knows who sent what message. It wasn't very professional but it was funny as hell and all the risqué propositions fit right in with the surrounding chaos. The boys loved it. They learned a lot about cattle and cattle trading, too.

That lesson was important since, as I mentioned, Cargill had acquired the world's largest cattle feed lot. I figured this was the real reason for the boys' visit so I described cattle grades (they already knew what "choice" meant!) and the contract deliverable specifications. In addition to hedging, Cargill would probably be taking or making delivery of live animals, not storable grains, something brand new to them so I explained another critical step. At the CME, you got a receipt representing the delivery of live cattle to one of the acceptable cattle feed areas around the country. I don't know if any of my guests used this information or ended up in the family business, but I do know their visit that day was educational in more ways than one. I learned something too. Just like the farmers from Iowa, Indiana, Wisconsin, and Illinois, Minnesota's all-American boys liked to laugh and have fun, fun, fun, fun, fun, which is a great actually, the only good job philosophy.

After we said goodbye and the day finally came to a close, Harvey, Vince and Cadillac Jack Schulte came to meet me and Pat Boyle for a drink at the Sign of the Trader. When the Sign closed, we moved onto Butch McGuires, and finally ended up at my penthouse in the sky. From my windows, we could see Ceres, the Goddess of Grains perched atop the CBOT. Thankful for her bounty, we toasted her with the guy's traditional toast "Tomorrow is another day, we will win, we will get them."

Chapter Six

JOY
MEMBER, CHICAGO BOARD OF TRADE

I bought my Chicago Board of Trade Financial Membership in May of 1977. My money was sparse, but my parents put my name on their house so my financial statement would show some assets. I also secured a loan that positioned me to purchase the $30,000 seat, now called an Associate Membership. With my funding in place, there was only one more hurdle – I had to be approved by a membership committee. Nervously, I went to be interviewed in the large boardroom. I was ready to jump through hoops, but the directors were so helpful and supportive that everything went well. I WAS IN! The acronym on my trading badge was JOY and that couldn't have been more accurate. After all, I'd been thinking about trading on my own for years and now the moment had finally arrived. I was thrilled but was I ready?

I remember kidding around with my sisters Gerri and Linda. I would ask them "how do I become one of the guys?" Then I'd start singing this old Peter, Paul and Mary song:

"I'll tie back my hair
Men's clothing I'll put on
I will pass as your comrade
As we march along."

Immediately, Linda said "forget it! You look so beautiful with your hair tied back that you'll never look like a man."

She was right. Besides, I was smart enough to know I would never be one of them so I didn't even try.

With that in mind, I left the security blanket of Cargill Investor Services a month later in June, 1977, but not before something odd happened. A few months before I departed, a new account came across my desk. It was a numbered trust account from a broker in Omaha, Nebraska - someone outside our organization. I back-tracked the wire transfer and to my shock, discovered that it had come from Imelda Marcos in the Philippines. The actual checks were generated by two high-ranking commanders, one, a member of the Viet Cong, the other, an officer in the Chinese Red Army. The account was supposed to hedge silver against sugar purchases. Flabbergasted, I immediately went to Dan Amstutz, then president of CIS. "You don't want this account," I insisted, handing him the information. I didn't need to say another word because the information I showed him spoke for itself.

Imelda Marcos was a hedger in sugar, not silver. While it isn't illegal to trade silver for sugar, it is BIG TIME illegal to claim to be a silver hedger if you are not. A hedger actually has the crops or the grains or the silver in hand. This is different than hedging a speculative position which means putting on a future position to protect your price, one reason the IMM is so important. True hedgers are allowed to carry a larger position than a speculator. While Marcos was a hedger in sugar, she was truly a speculator in silver. And we would truly be in trouble if we touched this account.

How had I figured it out, Dan wanted to know. Feminine intuition, I answered, along with some hard investigative work. The account was gone the next day. Why was this so important?

When a market is cornered by a group of people, acts of collusion can easily occur but proving it is hard. I didn't want anybody on my books who could possibly be accused of such illegal antics. Although I never told anyone, this case became my client barometer. In other words, I used this knowledge on the floor to find and assess good, honest customers for whom to trade gold, silver and financial contracts. Dan backed me 1000% and set a great professional example. Although he died in 2006, the guy had a spectacular career. After CIS, he became

Under Secretary of Agriculture, playing a prominent role during negotiations of the Uruguay Round of General Agreement on Tariffs and Trade rules for agriculture and on the U.S. occupation of Iraq. Working with him was like getting an MBA and even though he was a stern man of few words, I liked Dan a lot. He rarely smiled, but I coaxed several grins out of him because Dan enjoyed my brains and respected my balls. We discussed both frequently since he would pick me up in front of my house and we'd ride down to the CBOT together practically every day.

Dan's insights served me especially well when I headed onto the trading floor to begin my new career as a solicitor, broker, and trader, working on my own. Brokers and traders are the two types of members found in the pit. Brokers fill customer or arbitrage orders. Traders are locals trading for themselves. As a broker handling customer accounts, the first thing you have to do, of course, is get customers. Easy, right? Right - like building the Great Wall of China by hand. This was especially true since, at that moment, the Government National Mortgage Association Bonds (GNMA/Ginnie-Mae's) was the only existing financial contract available to trade or hedge. These were Government Bonds made up of mortgages on home loans bundled into units of $100,000.

As I studied trading Ginnie-Maes, John "BUD" Frazier, Vice Chairman of CBOT, offered me a job with the Clayton Brokerage Company out of St. Louis, Missouri. Bud was a big grain customer broker and most of the large grain companies traded through him including several Japanese and Brazilian clients. He was also hard to say "no" to so of course, I said yes.

My desk at Clayton Brokerage was right next to the silver pit where I could observe all the action. In 1977, when I bought my membership, there was only one other active female pit broker. Her name was Patti Lombardo. As a broker, she was in the pit all day long, filling her company's orders and arbitrage. Patti was a great gal and the guys really liked her. Another woman, Carol Ovitz Hancock, a CBOT member, position traded in grains and usually walked around the floor, but Patti was right in the thick of things. Once, her male pit mates presented Patti with a gift, a round badge that said I'VE GOT BALLS! As they pinned it on her jacket, they said "Patti, now you're one of us." The phrase was also a favorite of tennis great Billie Jean King and it was such a popular sentiment that once, when things got wild and the badge fell off her jacket, trading in the pit actually stopped while everyone searched for Patti's badge.

Now one of Patti's colleagues in the silver pit was C.C. Odom. He was - and is - a long, tall, Texan, six foot five, big, husky, and a real looker. A CBOT director for many years, C.C. is now a director of the CME Group. He is also bright, classy, and a real gentleman, traits that are rare in business. They are also exactly the qualities that helped keep things sane when the silver pit went wild. C.C.'s largest customer was the largest silver trader in the world, the Hunts of Texas. Nelson Bunker Hunt and his brother, William Herbert Hunt, both former billionaires, ran an oil dynasty and first started accumulating silver in the early 1970s. From 1978 to 1982, the brothers were the number one silver traders on the planet and by 1979, had practically cornered the global market, earning an estimated two to four billion dollars in silver speculation as prices skyrocketed from eight dollars an ounce to fifty dollars an ounce. But their fortunes came crashing down in 1989, when the Hunts became the hunted and the Commodity Futures Trading Commission charged Nelson with conspiring to manipulate and corner the silver market. They fined him ten million dollars and forbade him from trading in the commodity markets during his lifetime.

While the Hunt's story was very public, another CBOT episode was shrouded in mystery and remains so to this day. It happened in the fall of 1977, at the beginning of the gold and silver rally. Ralph Peters, a renowned silver trader and later, Chairman of the Chicago Board of Trade, experienced every parent's worst nightmare - his twenty-two year old daughter, Eleanor, vanished without a trace. On break from her studies at Vassar College, Eleanor was living in the Bahamas but on this particular occasion, she was staying with friends in Tampa Bay, Florida. On September 14 at 10:30AM, those friends dropped Eleanor off at the University of South Florida Golf Course for a two mile jog. But she never returned, and after twelve hours, her friends called the police.

Eleanor's disappearance was splashed across the front page of every Chicago paper as a dozen local detectives flew down to Florida to help with the search. Strangely, they returned the next day, then just as eerily, the newspapers went silent. You see, Eleanor, the great, great granddaughter of Reuben H. Donnelley was heir to the massive R.H. Donnelly Publishing fortune (now Dex One) which publishes the Yellow Pages and other related resources.

Three weeks later, on October 6, 1977, a man gathering wood stumbled across her badly decomposed body in a remote, forested area just three hundred yards off the golf course.

"...under the circumstances, it is naturally presumed foul play was involved," Dr. Peter Lardizabal, the Hillsborough (Tampa) County medical examiner told the Chicago Tribune and other newspapers. "This is a very suspicious case," Lardizabal continued, "...the girl was found fully clothed, lying face up not far from a road on a white sheet that partly covered her. Curiously, her shoes had been removed and neatly placed four inches from her feet." In addition, the young heiress' face was looking skyward and rumor had it that there was a ritualistic aspect to the scene. "It was made to look like she'd laid down and gone to sleep," Dr. Lardizabal theorized - but he was at a loss to explain the cause of death since the initial autopsy was inconclusive.

On the trading floor there were plenty of theories, founded and unfounded. Many of the stories contradicted each other, but as the weeks went by, they all grew increasingly dark. There were whispers about kidnapping, blackmail, international intrigue, and no wonder. It was the beginning of the fastest run in silver prices the world had ever seen and Ralph Peters, Eleanor's father, was one of the biggest silver players on the planet. We were terrified for him and for ourselves, partly because everything was so hush-hush and hushed was the operative word because the story evaporated from the headlines as fast as it came.

Today the crime remains unsolved; the cause of death a matter of debate; the motive - unknown; and the rumor mill still churns with speculation since the murder happened just as the gold and silver markets began to rumble. Did I say rumble? It was more like worlds colliding with fantastic runs, historically high prices, and near suicidal collapse. Think about it. In 1977, when Eleanor Peters died, silver was at $4.00, by 1979 it was $8.00, and by 1980, when the Hunts and Imelda Marcos were trading, silver catapulted to $48.00 an ounce. Simultaneously, gold became the hottest commodity in town - not just hot, but sizzling. From 1978 to 1980, gold brokers were in great demand, but the market was very volatile so you really had to know your stuff. Fortunately, I did.

I opened one large account and several smaller ones. Figuring that the high would be $800 (and I didn't want anybody on my books when it got there), I informed everyone that I wanted all positions liquidated when gold hit $756. What I hadn't figured on was this - suddenly, I, Joyce Selander, was in control of one-third of the open interest (the number of contracts outstanding between market participants at the close of each business day) at the Chicago Board of Trade. Holy shit!

It was huge, so huge that my percentage was dangerous for my customers. Immediately, I did the responsible thing and started putting positions on at the Chicago Mercantile Exchange. The CME had a contract based on one hundred troy ounces, similar to the CBOT contracts which were based on three kilos of gold. When gold traded up and through $750, the CBOT, the CME, in fact the whole trading world went insane! This was uncharted territory. How high would gold go? I wasn't going to stick around to find out.

I started liquidating positions and taking profits for my customers, just like I said I would. And my customers needed no prompting. One called and said "get me out of here now at $750!" Immediately, I called the CME floor and entered his order to sell at $750 or better. At that particular moment, the market was at $756 and moving fast toward Limit Up. "Limit Up" is a technical term that refers to the maximum amount the market is allowed to trade up (or down) each day and each day has its own Limit Up or Limit Down parameters. The exchanges set these parameters based on the previous night's close. For CBOT, CME, and the New York Mercantile Exchange, Limit Up stops higher trading. When the limit is touched, the market trades at that price and cannot trade any higher. When I sold and filled my customer's order the market was locked Limit Up. Locked limit up means that the standing bid is the highest price allowed to trade on that day. On that particular day, Limit Up should have been between $756 and $760, but the fill given to me was only $750! I screamed at the desk manager. The market was trading at $756 when I entered my customer's liquidation order and I wanted my fill at that price or better. I was going hoarse as I informed him in no uncertain terms that time and sales would back my price even though it was a fast market.

"Time and Sales" refers to two things - the order entry time physically stamped on the order and the confirmation-of-sale-price-at-the-time stamp. This is critical because during a fast market, there's sort of a controlled and sometimes not-so-controlled hysteria. All that excitement means that sometimes trades can be erratic. Like now. As the broker heatedly argued with me on the price, I got into his face. I KNEW the market never traded below $756 after I entered my customer's liquidating order. I had to protect my client and my reputation so I pulled out all the stops.

"I am a Member of the Board of Trade," I informed the trader via the desk clerk. "I want my fill at $756 or by ten minutes after the close I WILL BE SITTING ON CHAIRMAN LEO MELAMED'S KNEE PUTTING IN A FORMAL COMPLAINT! The damn price was obviously written incorrectly on the order. Fix it now!" I demanded, "or I will see you in arbitration."

Disbelieving, the broker turned to the desk manager. "Would she really do that?" he asked incredulously.

I batted my false eyelashes and smiled as instantly, miraculously, my client's order was corrected to $756. Why was this so important? Not only to protect my customer's position and my own reputation, but to protect the integrity of our industry. You see, that six dollar price difference was on a one hundred troy ounce contract. With gold trading at $756 an ounce, that meant there was a six hundred dollar price difference per contract and my client had five contracts. Bottom line, without the correction my customer would've been out $3000. $3000 might not sound like much, but to me (and my clients). every penny counts. More than that, if our industry is going to survive and thrive, our relationships have to be built on trust. Recent history has shown us what happens when that trust is violated - it doesn't just impact one trader and one client, it impacts the whole country and eventually, the whole world.

And that world was about to be ROCKED! It was in the middle of those mind-blowing gold and silver highs, within a day or two of my liquidations, and three years after Eleanor's death that her father, Ralph Peters, the mega-silver trader walked onto the floor. I swear a hush fell over the giant four-story room. As a trader, Ralph didn't handle customers and he rarely entered the pits because he knew everyone was watching him. He was right - thousands of people momentarily froze in their tracks to see what he would do. But not me. I knew what was coming and I dived for the phone. I reached my last remaining gold customer and whispered "we're getting out of your position NOW!" He'd bought it at $500. We sold it at $800. Then I called my Dad and told him to unload all the silver and silver coins we'd been hoarding. Dad sold at $48 an ounce, a price I doubt we'll see again. Hot damn! Both men were happy and so was I.

It was just in the nick of time, too. In what looked like slow motion, Ralph entered the silver pit, put both hands in the air with his palms facing outward toward the pit and said, "Sell silver. Sell silver LIMIT DOWN!" Chaos erupted. He was the King of the Mountain, in control, and selling the market short to deliver his silver.

Ralph had just thrown down the gauntlet, taking on the Hunts of Texas and everybody else who'd cornered the market and caused huge distortions in gold and silver prices. Some of these individuals were trading sugar for silver and the Commodity Futures Trading Commission was already actively investigating the Hunts. As for Ralph, it was common knowledge that he owned silver - lots of silver and lots of silver certificates. The certificates represented actual silver bars in vaults ready for immediate delivery on the CBOT and the New York Mercantile Exchange (NYMEX). Word of Ralph's action shot around the globe and prices plummeted. Based on the then, 5 day, Monday through Friday trading week, silver went limit down for thirty-three business days and gold went limit down for seventeen business days.

(Does this pattern seem familiar? Think back to crude oil, 2008, the spectacular run-up from sixty dollars a barrel in January, to one hundred fifty dollars in July, driven by Morgan Chase and Goldman Sachs with speculators driving it back down as low as $48 before it ended at $60 in December. Clearly, the Chicago temperatures weren't the only thing that plummeted as the crude oil market got cornered - just like silver.)

Of course, Ralph Peters, Silver King, knew exactly what he was doing on that day and any other. Since he owned silver bars outright, he'd made a fortune on both sides, buying and selling. When he sold, the market dropped fast because people were liquidating their long/buy positions so they would not have to take actual delivery of the bars. You see, when you trade commodities, you put up ten to twenty percent of the contract's value. When you actually take delivery, you pay 100% of that day's price. The price difference can be a problem - not just a problem, a catastrophe - so as a rule, customers don't want to take physical delivery of the bars. The rumor mill said Ralph had gotten out of all his commodity positions before he offered the market down limit, but his adversaries had not so some of them may have been forced to take actual delivery.

Now at that moment, there was a fortune in silver and gold sitting in the then active vault in the basement of the CBOT building. Depositing or withdrawing your silver bars or gold bullion worked like this. When you put them into the vault, a certificate would be issued representing the amount you had in storage. When you wanted delivery, you took your certificate back to the vault and withdrew the amount specified on the certificate - and this was no small undertaking.

The silver bars stored in the vault were the size of bricks. Trucks would pull up and depending on whether they were loading or unloading, the drivers would just throw the bricks into the back of their vehicles or pile them up on a cart and wheel them into the vault.

Whenever I watched this process, I wished I'd brought my little vacuum to suck up all the gold and silver dust because there was plenty of it.

And there was plenty of action at the CBOT as the gold and silver markets started moving up again along with inflation and interest rates. At that moment, summer of 1977, Government National Mortgage Association Bonds (GNMA) was the only financial contract available to trade or hedge. These were Government Bonds made up of mortgages on home loans bundled into units of 100,000 and all my U.S. and Municipal Bond traders were speculating on these so-called Ginnie-Mae's. Since they were all speculating on interest rates in the mortgage area, I spent most of my working hours in this particular pit, but there was something else on the horizon.

The U.S. Bond contract was set to open in Fall, 1977. My customers were getting ready and so was I. Every day when I finished my stint in the pit, I went on a long hunt for new bond accounts. Little did I know those twelve hour days and the Ginnie Mae's would help me make a bit of history. I didn't even think about it until I was at a big party in Lake Geneva, Wisconsin, where my friend, Stuart Ellison, a CBOT member, introduced me as the first woman in the world to physically trade financial futures at the Chicago Board of Trade.

At the time I laughed. "Stuart," I said, "that 's a slight exaggeration." But it wasn't.

I was the only woman trading Ginnie-Mae's. This made me the first woman in the first financial pit. When the next financial pit, the bond contract opened in September, 1977, several other women quickly joined me to physically trade financial futures. A great feminine camaraderie developed and we dubbed ourselves the Bondettes because we were strong, smart, and while we liked our martinis shaken, we were always rock solid professionals.

Chapter Seven

MY BIG ACCOUNT

One night, I was sitting in my neighborhood bar, Butch McGuires, waiting to meet my buddies, Butch - the place's namesake and owner - and Billy O'Connor, both exchange members. (Butch owned a CBOE seat thanks to his best friend, Billy.) While I was waiting, a Cash Euro Dollar trader who was a friend of my ex-fiancée walked in and joined me for a drink. His name was Ric Shanahan. Ric and I were talking about the new bond contract when Jim Behrens, a CBOT Financial member and dear friend of mine entered the room. Spotting Jim, Ric waved him over. "Jim is so lucky," Ric winked admiringly, "the guy is hung like a horse and every girl in town wants to sleep with him."

"You're wrong," coyly, I batted my false eyelashes. "It's Jim's college roommate, my ex-fiancée, Doug, who is so well-endowed."

Ric shook his head. "Ten-thousand dollars says you're wrong."

"Oh it was Doug," I said knowingly, "he was the desirable one and I refuse to take your money because I know I'm right."

Confident, Ric strolled over to ask Jim THE QUESTION.

Laughing, eyeing me over Ric's shoulder, Jim shook his head "No," and verified that it was my ex-, Doug, who was hung like a stallion. Immediately, Ric walked back and offered me ten thousand dollars.

"No way!" I laughed, "I tried to warn you."

Ric grinned. "Ok Joyce, but instead I'm going to send a giant bond account your way." True to his word, Ric called the next day and passed on the name and private phone number of this big trader, a wild Irishman from New York. I set up the meeting and got ready to fly out to meet Tom Sullivan. I knew I was onto something huge because my partner, Bud Frazier, was so excited he could hardly keep his pants on.

And I definitely decided to keep my pants off, refusing to wear the tailored blue pants suit that is SOOO New York and would make me look like everybody else on Wall Street. But what should I wear instead? Hmm, wild and crazy Chicago trader that I am, I chose a full skirted white dress with medium sized blue flowers, a wide belt and high neck with a matching scarf tied in a large bow on my left shoulder. The skirt fell just below my knees and the whole ensemble made my confidence soar. I felt as great as I looked and I looked like I'd stepped right out of Vogue magazine. It helped that I'm petite, 5'5", 110 pounds, and wear a size 2 dress. I am also blonde, blue-eyed, and have a smile from heaven even if the day has been hell - my secret weapon, and exactly what Tom Sullivan and company weren't expecting.

As I waited patiently in the reception area of Tom's office, a sophisticated, silver-haired (read HOT!) man walked by. I gave him my best, big, beautiful, All-American smile and he smiled back. Before things could go any further, the receptionist said, "Mr. Sullivan will see you now." Nuts! Oh, well, I consoled myself, I was here on business.

I entered Tom's office. Just as I started my presentation, there was a knock on the door. Immediately, Tom excused himself and opened the door halfway, shielding the visitor from my view. But through the crack between the hinges, I could see that it was HIM, the silver-haired Adonis who'd smiled at me in the lobby. Tom was telling him that I was from CBOT, but Adonis cut him short.

"I don't care what she's selling, buy it!" Adonis ordered Tom.

I smiled to myself. Talk about dress for success! We made arrangements for Tom to open several accounts, with me promising to send the paperwork the very next day. As I sat in the limo Tom had booked to take me back to the airport, I could hardly contain my excitement. My first big bond account! My first big account from New York! I was practically walking on air as I passed an airport newspaper vendor filling the racks of his kiosk with the current issue of Time magazine. There on the cover was the good-looking, silver haired Adonis whose name I didn't know. Immediately, I bought a copy.

The next morning I set the Time article smack, dab in the middle of my partner Bud's desk. Bud practically did a back flip, jumped off his chair, and gave me a huge hug. Whoever said size doesn't matter was wrong. That bet on Jim's penis had just landed me my biggest account ever: Norton Simon and Company, a conglomerate of Hunt Wesson Foods, Max Factor, Avis, Canada Dry, Johnnie Walker Scotch, Avis, Halston and more.

I was on a roll, I thought, as I split my time between Norton Simon and my other accounts, including one in grains with the infamous Uncle Julius Frankel. He was older, a long-time CBOT member, and famous, influential cash grain trader who'd started speculating for himself. Julius knew the grain markets better than anyone on the floor and we'd been friends since I worked at Cargill and Conti where he had trading accounts. Julius put token trades through me or Bud Frazier at Clayton Brokerage to help me make a few commissions. He did that because Julius liked working with me professionally and because he adored women. All women.

In particular, Julius loved the young girl runners, the prettier, the better. He called them "dollies" and he liked to reward them in a very special way. Every Friday, Julius loaded one pocket with ten dollar bills and the other with twenties. If you said "Hello, Uncle Julius!" and gave him a kiss on the cheek, you got a ten or twenty dollar bill. While it might sound sleazy, it was actually very sweet. You see, Julius' wife had died young, in her mid-thirties, from cancer. Shortly after her death, their beloved French poodle died too. Childless, this double loss was overwhelming for Julius and it made him incredibly generous. Inspired by his wife's battle against the disease and by his nephew who was working in cancer research, Julius left large sums of money to various cancer research efforts. He also left money to Chicago's Near North Animal Hospital.

The Near North Animal Hospital has a special place in my heart because that's where my brother-in-law, Rich Nye, interned and met Uncle Julius. Does Rich's name sound familiar? He was a southpaw pitcher for the 1969 Chicago Cubs. Back in Rich's day, you had to have a career after sports (especially after the Cubs!) so Rich left baseball to become a Doctor of Veterinary Medicine. He and Julius had a great friendship and sometimes we would all go out for dinner. Julius would also join us for the Lyric Opera. He had coveted first or second row seats that operaphiles spend years waiting to acquire. He was also best friends with Ardis Krainik, Lyric's legendary general manager. They had a fantastic relationship and the Julius Frankel Foundation finances several operas a year in Ardis' memory.

Rich's friendship with Uncle Julius and, I'd like to think me, inspired him to become a member of the CME. He joined the exchange in 1980, trading Eurodollars in the morning and tending to his veterinary practice in the evenings and afternoons. Rich also backed up my other brother-in-law, Walter "Skeeter" Haller, who became a large floor broker in the Euro Dollar Pit. Through the gossip mill, I talked to a few brokers and learned that Skeeter wasn't making any broker commissions which was a strain on his budget. I also knew he was hungry to get business and make some money, so I made Skeeter leave t-bills for Euros because my buddy Ric Shanahan said they would be the biggest contract ever at the CME. I knew the banks would be approved to trade Euros on January 1, 1981, so I persuaded Skeeter to stick around for the big day. And it wasn't just big - it was stupendous. Skeeter couldn't even talk, he was so busy. After the close, he called and asked what I knew that nobody else did. What I knew was that the banks would start to trade January 1. I also knew that I was determined to be very supportive to Skeeter and Rich as they worked to expand their business. And I wanted to expand mine, too.

My next bond account was Kim Rellahan, a large Commercial Paper trader from Lehman Brothers, Chicago. (Commercial paper is a short term, promissory note issued by a corporation which pays a higher yield than a Treasury Bill.) Once the bond contract opened, Kim and every U.S. and municipal bond trader from Lehman wanted to speculate or hedge in bonds. As a result, I wound up trading for SEVENTEEN Lehman bond traders. They tried to coordinate their calls into one single order and sometimes it sounded like a sit-com. First,

Kim would say, "sell five at market, then make it seven." I would say "I sold ten and give me the account numbers." Then he would say "sell seven more for a total of seventeeen." Some of the Lehman guys would trade two or three contacts, others traded ten each. It changed everyday and really kept me hopping. They also gave me great insights into the thinking of other speculators which was very beneficial later, when I started speculating on my own. By thankful contrast, the majority of gold traders I dealt with were holding their positions because gold and silver prices were going up, as were interest rates. Because things were a little quieter on the gold side, this made it easier for me to keep track of the bond traders, most of whom traded during the day.

Sometimes I would hand signal their trades to my pit broker, Michael Forbeck. Other times, I filled the order myself because speed was of the essence. My partner, Bud Frazier, preferred that I use the pit brokers to avoid risk and he was right. If something went wrong creating an out trade error it could cost me money that would immediately come out of my cash error account. So, for a small fee, I passed the risk onto my pit broker. He would physically trade the order for me inside the pit and be responsible for a correct fill. If something went wrong he had to deal with it, not me. I worked with Lehman's traders for about a year when they finally opened their own floor operations, but by then, I'd come to a major decision - I wanted to stop trading for customers and enter the pit full-time to start trading for myself, alone. Did I have what it takes to go into hand-to-hand financial combat in the pits and come out a winner? It was time to find out. I figured the odds were in my favor because I was fast, because I could take advantage of being physically in the pit, and most of all, because I was totally passionate about trading. Besides, it was the only way to become Queen of the Mountain.

Chapter Eight

THE TRADING PIT

What was it like, this life in the pits?

In 1982, the largest pit at the Chicago Board of Trade was the U.S. Treasury Long Term Bond. Physically, the bond pit was round with four steps leading from the floor level up to the top of the pit and six steps leading from the top level down to the pit's center. The center of the pit (they're all this way) was under floor level so the desks had a clear view of the action. The Long-Term Bond pit held approximately five hundred traders and at least six hundred broker's assistants who fell under the general title of clerks. Some clerks stood around the edge of the pit on the four upper steps and from that position, they quoted markets. Several hundred more clerks ran orders in and out while still others did trade checking. Brokers stood on the top step and big traders were one step down on step two. All day long we jostled for position, sweated, were hyped on testosterone and at least a little estrogen (mine!) as we stood pore-to-pore. Talk about getting to know your neighbor! The pit has been enlarged several times since its inception, but with so many people crowded into one space, it never seemed big enough. Maybe that's because things were constantly in motion with people trading bonds and putting it all on the line day after day. It was truly financial combat and this gladiators' arena was my happy home for seven years.

I stood on the second step inside the pit. This was my spot, my hard-won turf. If you came too close, I made sure you got to meet my forearm. Above me, on the very top step of the bond pit, was our "nosebleed section," reserved for Floor Brokers only. These brokers filled customer and proprietary arbitrage orders. The orders could be printed, hand-written, verbal, or communicated by hand signals from the trading desks. The desks were like nerve centers and a lot of brokers or their clerks wore headsets so they could speak directly to their desks and international offices as they traded throughout the day. With me on the second step were the large traders and scalpers (traders who are willing to continuously buy the bid or sell the offer). The rest of the steps leading down to the center of the pit were arranged in a hierarchy of importance, seniority, and timing. In other words, most of the top step was reserved for the closest delivery month, called the lead month and this was where the main contract trading by volume took place. The next trading month was on the other side of the pit and six months out would be in the center with the spread brokers.

A spread is a simultaneous trade where you buy one month and sell another month. In grains, this might mean buying old crop such as grain in storage, against selling a new crop that has just been planted taking into account the vagaries of weather and the amount of acreage planted. In Financials, a spread is two different bond yields. Spreading is used by speculators or hedgers who believe there will be a change in interest rates from one year to another or short term rates vs. long term rates affecting the yield curve.

An actual trade worked like this. A clerk on the outside steps of the pit would use hand signals to relay the bids and offers being screamed inside the pit to their firm's trading desks. In addition, the clerks received buy/sell hand signals from their firms or customers and would verbally relay these orders as well. The brokers endorsed the trading cards and orders of executed trades -called fills - which were then returned to the desk by a runner. If a clerk made an error, it was up to his or her boss to correct it.

Sound confusing? It looks even worse. One man actually referred to the process as organized insanity and daily pandemonium. He was right. But it's also correct to say that the system is efficient, not just efficient, but thrilling. The chorus of people screaming and yelling during a busy market was – is – sheer, high-octane adrenaline and energy that inspired me and kept me going. Of course, it could also drive you crazy. Some days you had to leave the pit – even leave the floor – to regain your sanity. Of course, the good days outnumbered the bad and that lured me back again and again.

So did the sheer challenge of the financial markets. The U.S. Long Bond opened in September, 1977, on the old Chicago Board Options Exchange (CBOE) trading floor with an average daily volume of 28,000 contracts. It was – and still is – the largest new contract trading volume ever achieved. In fact, that number was so huge and the original pit was so small that after a couple of weeks, we outgrew the trading area.

The second largest trading pit was almost as crowded. That was the Euro Dollar at the Chicago Mercantile Exchange. This pit was shaped like a long boat – appropriate since its occupants had apparently all learned their manners from ancient Vikings. The guys even looked like Vikings with an average height of 6'5", hulking good looks, and a talent for marauding. I used to call it the "Ship of Fools" – just kidding – but it was hard to miss the similarities.

The CME was in a separate building five or six blocks from the Chicago Board of Trade. I had memberships in both exchanges. At the CME, I held an agricultural membership. At the CBOT, I had a financial associate membership. Now my company's main trading desk was on the CBOT floor – a football field's distance from my partner, Bud. Maybe more than a football field because the trading floor is huge, so huge that people are always shocked at its size. One day, as I worked my way toward Bud, I decided to walk a customer order over to the soybean oil pit.

As I passed soybeans (not to be confused with soybean oil) I couldn't resist waving at handsome Chuck Wafer who was standing on the top step. Beside him was Archie Ryman, a genuine comedian and very funny character. The commodity business actually produced a lot of funny characters, maybe because there were lots of superstitions that led to some very strange behaviors. Like this one. When the soybean pit wanted the price to go up, Archie would start singing his favorite song – "Brazil, cha cha… cha cha cha cha, there are no soybeans in Brazil, cha cha... cha cha cha cha." The song didn't always work, but it did create a little humor on a lackluster day. Laughing at Archie's serenade, I hastened my steps toward soybean oil, CBOT's smallest pit.

When I reached my destination, I climbed to the top to talk to the broker. Suddenly, Ron Young, my former boss at Conti Commodities and Vice President of the CBOT entered the pit. He was filling a crush order. A crush is a three-legged spread. That meant Ron was buying soybeans and selling soybean oil and soybean meal.

Ooops! My CBOT membership allowed me to trade financial contracts, but technically, I wasn't allowed access to the grain pits here and Ron knew it.

He looked me up and down, then said jokingly "what are you doing in the oil pit?"

"I'm on my way to the bathroom," I smiled sweetly, pointing to the men's room.

The whole pit burst into laughter. "I won't touch that line," Ron grinned as he filled his crush spread.

You see, at that time there was no Women Members' bathroom anywhere on the exchange floor while the Men Members' bathroom was right next to the oil pit. To go to the ladies room, I had to climb a flight of stairs, trek through the members' coffee shop, traverse the Visitors' Gallery and use the restroom intended for female tourists. Shockingly, it would be several years before there was a womens' bathroom on the exchange floor. It took until April, 1982, when our bond pit moved into the grain room that a ladies facility was finally nearby.

Speaking of moving, bonds eventually took over the Soybean pit and the exchange had to enlarge the area two more times to accommodate all the action. And I decided I was ready to move into that action in a big way. In 1979, I gave up my customer business to enter the pit and trade for myself full-time. It was what I 'd always wanted to do - trading my own account, making my own money. I was home.

Every day I'd arrive at the pit at 7AM to hold my spot until the opening bell rang at eight. By contrast, my good friend, John J. O'Doherty (with whom I shared my spot for years) would arrive at 7:55.

Husky, 6'3", and a good-looking Irishman, J.J. was my best friend and protector in this gladiators' arena. It was appropriate too, because he had the body of a Roman god with a broad muscular chest, thick neck, cute firm ass, and massive rock hard thighs - which is why I christened him Thunder Thighs. Thunder Thighs also had a deep, sonorous voice, dark eyes and hair that curled when he sweated - which was most of the time. We all sweated, because trading was intellectually stressful and extremely physical, so physical that the combined body heat in the room often raised the floor temperature five to ten degrees and sent the pit temperature up by twenty degrees or more. Hell, just looking at J.J. could raise my temperature and a lot of other females felt the same way. Fortunately, J.J. loved women and he took good care of us, especially me.

Every day I literally stood between his legs with his body tightly pressed against mine. Before opening, the temperature was already 90 degrees and the minute the bell rang, it mercilessly went up as the pit baked with people on top of people. Within five minutes I would be dripping with J.J.'s sweat. I bitched at him daily, telling him to wear cotton underwear, but J.J. just laughed and kept sweating all over me. Between the heat and people spitting in your face, keeping my make-up on was next to impossible. My false eyelashes just melted off. And couture clothing? Forget it. I had to replace it (on the floor anyway) with cotton blouses. Do you know how hard it is to find a one hundred percent cotton blouse? But the sweat lodge was worth it because with J.J. it was always a hot, physical enjoyable session - I mean trading, of course!

In the members' coffee shop there was a small section that looked down on the sweaty bond pit. A bunch of us would hang out there and chat while watching the market right below us. One day we were debating football when Jack Carter (then President Jimmy Carter's son) said "Careful, Joyce knows football. After all, she's dated a whole football team."

"Not the whole team," I corrected him, "I usually date line men and I've never dated a quarterback."

"What about Bobby Douglas?" Jack teased me.

"Oh, I forgot about him." I exclaimed.

Jack then proceeded to name a cornerback from the Vikings who I was positive no one knew about.

I stared at him. "What did you do? Run a Secret Service check on me? "

"No," Jack laughed.

Just then I looked at the bond pit and saw a White House-based Secret Service agent standing there. "Jack," I said, "Your daddy's here. There's one of his advance agents by the pit." (I knew this because White House agents tend to be physically bigger and look more intimidating than other members of the service. Plus, they all wear small pins on their lapels in exactly the same position, something I'd learned from Denny.)

But Jack just laughed.

"No, Jack, I'm serious!"

Jack started to say his mom, Rosalynn, might come by but suddenly he stopped, jumped up and tore down the back stairs toward the pit.

We all ran after him. There, standing on the walkway above the pit were President and Mrs. Carter. Jack's proud parents. Like any other proud parents in the world.

Ah yes, I smiled to myself, just another day in the pits.

Chapter Nine

BIMBOS, LIMOS, AND LINES

In the early eighties, cocaine hit Chicago - especially the financial community - in a big way. It seemed like everyone was doing it - except me. I have always been very anti-drug and daily I bitched about the drug use around me. This is partly because I'm luckily and fortuitously allergic to codeine, penicillin, bactrin, sulfa, eggs and all derivatives of these substances so NO COCAINE FOR ME! Besides, I like to be in control of my life and that was hard enough in the increasingly hyperactive pits.

And the pits were increasingly hyperactive because too many people were using cocaine. There were constant, after work parties and everybody from the lowest clerks to some top rung executives were doing lines of the drug. You could tell by their behavior. Cocaine hypes you up and makes you feisty, gives you an adrenaline rush and makes you sweat - just like the market. It was a situational overdose and the mixture was violent - no surprise since cocaine is a violent drug.

Fights broke out in the pit practically every day as the ammonia-like smell of cocaine filled the air. Sometimes it was so pungent, so pervasive that I swore I could taste it on my lips and that revolted me. What revolted me even more was the drug's grip, the need to get high again and again, and the horror of people coming down - because I saw too many who never got back up.

Cocaine and the pits were a bad mix, and I constantly bitched at J.J. about coke. One day I told him "first you have trouble getting it up, then you can't get it up, then the damn thing falls off."

The guy standing next to J.J. said, "Why do you put up with her?"

"I'd rather have her between my legs than you, any day," J.J. replied. There was a moment of silence, then J.J. whispered in my ear. "I didn't mean that the way it came out."

But I just laughed. J.J. really adored me and he cared about my feelings. How lucky was I?

J.J. and I had a good friend, in fact, J.J.'s best friend, Mike Forbeck, 24, who had an escalating drug problem. Mike was doing way too much cocaine and to make matters worse, he was popping Quaaludes to manage the hypertension the cocaine brought on. His mood swings were more pronounced each day with the highs getting higher and the lows getting lower. J.J. and I were both worried about him. We didn't realize it at the time, but Mike was chronically depressed. We were concerned personally because we cared about the guy, and professionally because he was my bond floor broker and a damn good one. Mike filled customer orders for other clearing houses too and was considered a natural, totally at home in the pit.

Maybe it was genetic. Mike's father was a large filling broker in the corn complex and a partner at a major clearing firm. He, like a lot of people in our business, had a summer place in Lake Geneva, Wisconsin, about ninety minutes north of Chicago. J.J. and Mike would go there every weekend to boat and golf, rejuvenate and enjoy family parties. In fact, there seemed to be nonstop Lake Geneva parties every weekend throughout the summer.

And the partying wasn't confined to weekends. One day after work, a fellow trader, Heather, invited J.J., Mike and I over to use her pool. I had just returned from Acapulco so I was tanned and looking hot in my new blue Norma Kamali one piece bathing suit. I changed clothes at Heather's condo and walked out of the bedroom. Mike took one look at me and his jaw hit the floor. He said his ex-girlfriend had the same suit in red.

"That's funny," I said, "I saw a girl from Chicago in Acapulco. She was wearing a red suit just like mine."

Mike and J.J. exploded. What was all the fuss about? Then I found out the girlfriend had just broken up with Mike, absconded with his checkbook, and headed for Mexico. There under the hot sun, she was spending his money muy rapido and looked ecstatic doing it. Talk about retail therapy! I told J.J. and Mike everything I knew including descriptions of the people she was with and the places where she was hanging out. The next day, J.J. caught a flight to Acapulco to find her. Unfortunately, he had no luck and couldn't even track down anyone who remembered seeing her.

For Mike it was the last straw. The break up and the pressures of the market were too much, plus, the cocaine was destroying the sweet, gentle person he truly was. There was a great innocence about Mike and the ugly aspects of life made no sense to him, even though I tried to explain. You see, I was kind of like Mike's big sister, or maybe, a substitute for the mother he could never talk to. I sensed that Michael wanted me to save him, but he didn't make it easy. Correction, the cocaine and depression didn't make it easy.

I'll never forget the trading day when Mike got right in my face screaming "fuck!" Then his eyes welled up with tears. "I'm so sorry, I didn't mean to say that to you," he apologized.

"I know, sweetie," I replied, "it's okay." For Mike to speak to me that way was totally out of character and though it took me by surprise, I reacted with good grace. Still, his behavior worried me and when I look back, I now see that Mike was starting to lose it in a big way.

It was the weekend before the Fourth of July holiday. Mike was extremely depressed and had started to call me every night. I took all his calls and never hung up even though his distress saddened me so. On this particular night he was talking even more strangely than usual and saying he didn't want to live anymore. I didn't know what to say, but I tried to listen. I could see cocaine had this good man in its grip. He was deteriorating before my very eyes and it was terrifying.

On Friday after the close, we met for a cocktail and Mike told me he'd lost thirty thousand dollars in the market that day. I tried to comfort him, advising him not to worry about it. After all, in the greater scheme of things, it wasn't that much money and he would make it back next week. I had to go, and reluctant, I left him at the Sign of the Trader with a promise that we would continue our conversation Tuesday morning, after the 4th of July holiday. I reminded him not to dwell on things, wished him well, and told him to have a great time over the weekend. Then I rushed out because I was leaving for a wedding in New Orleans and would just make my plane.

Before I left the building I ran into J.J. and warned him to watch over Mike that weekend in Lake Geneva. I tried to impress on J.J. how worried I was about Mike's state of mind, but J.J. said, "I'm not his keeper. Mike's a big boy. He can take care of himself."

And he did.

That weekend, Mike didn't go to Lake Geneva. Instead, our sweet little brother put a gun to his head and blew his brains out.

It was the first news I heard when I arrived back on Tuesday. Shaking, I climbed into the pit. After a three day holiday weekend, the market was crazy and I had a position so I had to stay all day and trade but it was torture. With J.J. at my back, I cried and cried. J.J. cried and cried too and we did not speak. This went on for two days. On the third day, we finally screamed at each other, cried some more, and finally fell into each other's arms, hugging as close and tight as we could. Our hearts were broken. Our sweet little brother, Michael, was gone. And there still isn't closure.

Because of the circumstances, Michael's family had a private funeral service so I never got to say goodbye. That haunts me still, and I still have not visited Michael's grave because the pain is too great. In fact, right now, as I write this, I am sobbing uncontrollably. It's been almost thirty years and Mike was so young, so gorgeous, and so full of life. I miss him and I always will.

There are other people I miss, too. Shortly after Michael's death, two friends in the bond pit died of drug abuse. And drugs killed my love life. I broke up with my stud muffin, Dean, because he loved cocaine more than he loved me. I hated drugs then and I hate them today. The price is too high when you trade a lifetime of potential and joy for a line of white powder that wipes out the past, the present, and the future. Especially the future since I had wanted all of us to grow old together but stay young at heart.

Barry Lind, the first love of my life understood this well. As the first commodity trader interviewed by Time Magazine, Barry said "Commodity Trading makes you grow old fast but keeps you young forever." And Barry was living proof. So, I hope, am I.

We are two of the lucky ones who not only survived but thrived, and it wasn't easy because trading isn't easy. It isn't all fast money, fun and games. The stress is a high price to pay. Many days, I walked out the CBOT door in tears, so battered and beaten I could hardly move. I was constantly getting hit or kicked. I always had black and blue bruises on my body and sometimes, my soul. No, there is nothing easy about life in the pit.

Chapter Ten

MY DAD

Sometimes I stop and wonder where the gifts came from -- this ability to survive in an insane, high pressure business and the fearlessness that allowed me to press on and pursue success while staying true to my values and my authentic self. The answer is my parents. I know my inner drive comes from the great love they had for me and the rough times they experienced when they were young.

During World War II, my dad was shipped off to Germany. My mom was alone with a ten month old baby when she discovered she was pregnant with me. My mom was sick and had taken a new medication that made her violently ill. Throwing up for days along with abdominal and intestinal cramps and bleeding. The doctors were sure she had had a miscarriage, but here I am. Months later, mom received a telegram telling her my dad was missing-in-action and presumed dead. But instead of being devastated like most women, she held her head high and said "my baby is still alive and I know my husband is, too." She kept the faith, counting the days until he came home.

But there were many days that homecoming was in doubt. As my dad later put it, he was the first man on and off Normandy Beach. You see, he was one of two scouts sent ahead to check the beach before the Allied forces landed. The other scout went to the right. My dad went to the left, running into a wooded area. From this high point, he could see Germans surrounding the beach. Lightning fast, Dad sprinted toward the shore, but he was too late. Most of the American troops had already landed and were headed up the sand, straight toward the waiting enemy. Dad screamed a warning, shouting for the men to follow him as Nazi fire pounded down. But the sound was deafening as gunfire and explosions filled the air and bodies collapsed all around him. Officers yelled for the soldiers to follow my dad and about a dozen troops ran after him toward the safety of the trees, but ultimately, only three men survived - including my father.

My dad and the others hid for two weeks as Germans scoured the beach looking for survivors. The trio lived off the food they found on dead bodies and on small animals they could kill with a knife. Dad was slightly injured but they managed to hold out until they were finally found by U.S. troops. My father was hospitalized for a time, but the field hospital patched him up and the brass sent him out to fight again.

Again he got injured this time by a hand grenade and the effects of the wound were lifelong. When I was little, I remember going into my parent's room and seeing blood all over the top sheet. I was hysterical until my dad said "Look, Joyce, it's just a small piece of metal sticking out of your papa's toe. Go get the tweezers and we will pull it out." Later in life, when my dad was in his mid-seventies, he experienced four cerebral hemorrhages. I always thought they were caused by small pieces of metal still traveling through his body. The staff at Veterans Hospital didn't disagree, on the other hand they didn't say I was right, but it sure makes sense to me.

One week before Memorial Day, 1995, on the fiftieth anniversary of WW II, the United States Army sent an officer to the Veterans Hospital where they presented my father with the medals he should have received half a century earlier including the Bronze Battle Star, the Purple Heart, the World War II Victory Medal, and The European Campaign Medal with One Bronze Star. Dad also received the Good Conduct Medal. Receiving the honors that should have been bestowed when he was discharged on December 4, 1945, seemed to give my father closure and he died later that Memorial Day weekend, leaving a legacy of bravery and love.

I remember that when I have a bad day. My problems in the pit were small compared with what my parents endured and any success I've had is a tribute to their courage, resilience, and heart, something I thank them for daily.

Chapter Eleven

1982 - A NEW FLOOR, NEW TRADERS, AND NEW OPPORTUNITIES

In 1982, the new CBOT trading floor was completed and with it, new opportunities and challenges arose. The bond pit was moved into the old soybean pit and although the pit had been enlarged, traders just kept coming! You see, over the last few years, interest rates had soared from 6% to 20% and they were now on the way down. When I took my seat loan out in 1977, I was paying 6 1/2%. That was one point above prime and my dad was concerned about my loan since rates had climbed to 8 1/2%. He asked me where I thought the rates were going and I said they would double. On hearing that, my father begged me to let him pay off the loan with the money he'd made in silver. I wanted to pay it off myself, but Dad had a point, so before rates hit 10%, I let him do it. Thank God I did. With less financial pressure, I started making more money and within six months, I was able to pay him back in full. How? I put the money in a t-bill yielding 18%. Now that's what you call volatility in interest rates.

And volatility was the name of the game since the new pit rapidly became more dangerous than its small, overcrowded predecessor in the south room. It was truly a gladiators' arena with traders battling daily in hand-to-hand combat. Since I am petite, most of the guys were quite protective of me, but my size didn't fool them. If they got in my face, they got a forearm to the throat! And vice versa. I was constantly bruised, covered with black and blue marks and spit. Yes, the unintentional spitting as people shouted orders was gross and the intense crowding made the potential for fainting high. I would yell, "I'm going to pass out!" whereupon the guys would move over and give me a few seconds worth of breathing room.

When I caught my breath and yelled that I was O.K., they moved back into their respective spots causing a huge wavelike effect as we repositioned ourselves. The wave was so big it would actually lift me off my feet and send me airborne. I'd actually have to slide down my neighbors until my feet touched the step. This was especially precarious since I'd lost my longtime protector, J.J., who had recently purchased a full membership and had decided to start trading grains.

With J.J. gone, I tried trading from different parts of the pit but it was always the same. You had to be near the orders to get the trades and make the money. That's why everyone was there. Now I never made a lot of money, but I didn't lose a lot either and that's the name of the game. Limit your losses. Take big profits and small losses and you will survive so I guess you would say I survived. Especially when I finally found a spot in the pit I actually liked.

It was in the second row, right in front of a big broker named John Bollero. John was about 5'10" and had an Italian look with blue eyes and brown hair on a slender frame. He had a sincere way of talking and was a highly experienced grain broker before coming into the bond room. John was also more in control than some of the other brokers – guys who were jumping all over the place, wildly swinging their arms, and just plain hazardous to stand by. That relaxed demeanor was why I liked him and why I was pretty sure he liked me standing in front of him. John especially liked that I was short and didn't obstruct his sight lines to the pit. He could easily see over me and to his right and left. This was important since he traded big quantities and needed room to execute his trades. (Brokers who are 6'5" don't have this problem!) John showed his appreciation by going out of his way to divide up his orders so there would be a little for me. It was like receiving John's blessing, something that came in handy one day when I ran into trouble in the pit.

I was standing in my usual spot trading when this bully starts pushing and knocks me off my step. My elbow hit the guy next to me in the eye and suddenly everyone was yelling and screaming like it was all my fault. The bully shouted that I didn't belong there but the truth was he and I traded at about the same amount so we were equal. Still, he refused to move over to let me back in my spot so I pushed my way in. John saw exactly what happened and when he received his next order, Sell 100 at the market, he divided it up as usual in 20, 20, 20, 20, 18 and 2 lots. Of course, the two lots were for me. Suddenly the bully said, "I want all twenty." Looking over my head at him John said "Joyce, honey, do you want 20?" I hesitated, then replied "two contracts are fine." John stared at the bully and said "eighteen lots, asshole." By this time the bully was practically foaming at the mouth. "I don't know why she has to stand here," he screamed. But everybody just stared at him and you could tell we were all thinking how stupid he was.

Unfortunately, that wasn't the end of it. Charlie Di Francesca, head of the pit floor conduct committee, told me to stay after the close. He began lecturing me as though the incident was all my doing. I'd had a rough day and started to cry when Ralph Goldenberg, Vice Chairman of CBOT and owner of the company I cleared my trades through walked by. "What's wrong?" he asked. I explained what had happened and Ralph said he'd take care of it.

Ralph immediately went to Freddie Bryzowksi, the owner of the Chicago White Sox, the Chicago Bulls, and the bully's clearing firm. The bully, said Ralph, pushed my little "JOYCEE!" That did it. Freddie told the bully not to go anywhere near me and ordered him to stand on the opposite side of the pit. The opposite side across from me was for second option and back months. They were not the areas where you stood to scalp, which was what the bully did. Taking pity on the guy, Freddie told him he could come back and stand near me whenever I said it was okay. Eventually, I told Mr. Bully he could return to my side of the pit but by then things weren't going so well for him. I suspect he was unable to rebound because soon he was gone. For awhile no one bothered me and the story become pit legend.

Another pit legend was the size of the new CBOT and this wasn't just legend, it was fact. The new room was huge - four stories high and the width of two football fields set side by side. The old CBOT room had held all the grain pits including soybeans, soybean oil, soybean meal, wheat, corn, oats and options contracts as well as the metals, silver and gold. At that time, there were several hundred trading desks on steps going up the walls and around the pits. There were also cash grain desks scattered throughout the floor and of course, that most important of all structures, the Men's Washroom.

The new room (that's CBOT, not the Men's Washroom although I suspect a lot of business was conducted in there!) held four main pits including the U.S. Treasury Long Term Bond, the Ten Year Note, the Municipal Bond, and the large Bond Option Pit with more financial markets soon to come. In fact, the financial markets had taken over as the main volume of the Chicago Board of Trade and with them, more members and trading desks than ever before. We finally had enough wall space to put up more quote boards than we had been able to fit in the old room. This was important because when you trade bonds, there are many daily and global economic factors to take into account. This information is critical since these economic indicators can control interest rates, the value of the dollar, and they change from minute to minute

To keep track of these changes, we had a live Reuter's newswire giving us real time updates of news and economic reports worldwide. The quote boards for stocks, options, and commodities including crude oil, gold, silver, and all the CBOT grains were updated moment by moment. In addition, we posted CME products like foreign currencies, eurodollars, cattle and hogs, and all the stock Indexes. We also had CRT screens strategically placed high above the trading pits. The screens quoted live trading in cash bonds, coupons, treasury notes and bill rates. Everything was right in front of us including, eventually, CNBC Financial news broadcasting on giant TV screens all day.

This was important because a huge movement in crude oil or a massive sale of grains will cause changes in interest rates, the dollar and foreign currencies. In other words, since all these prices and commodities interact, a change in one commodity has an effect on several others. The pricing of these goods can in turn impact the dollar against a foreign currency. In addition, the parties involved in these transactions risk a large price fluctuation. That's why these trades must be hedged in the futures market to protect both the buyer and the seller's price. (That's also why we watched crude oil prices so closely in the 80's, just like we did in 2008 and 2010.)

Successful buying and selling - trading - is all about information. Open out-cry, an important factor in the commodity markets, keeps information flowing to traders and brokers worldwide. While electronic trading has made the industry more accessible to more people, in my opinion, it has created too much secrecy, allowing banks and big companies to hide what they're doing in the open markets. By contrast, in open out-cry pits, the traders, companies, and their customers know immediately when a Morgan or a Goldman or some other large brokerage house starts buying or selling commodities like crude oil or gold. Nowadays, few, if any, get this information. Is that a good thing? Consider.

When we started trading bonds in 1977, the cash quote would be 99.00 to 99.16, a big spread, in part because transactions used to be handled on the phone without outsider knowledge. After the CBOT bond contract began trading in the open out-cry format, the price became 99.00 to 99.01. The bond contract put bids and offers in line thanks to speculators and scalpers in the pit. A scalper is willing to buy at one or sell at two, making one tick on the transaction which narrows the bid and offer spread. With the scalper in between the customers and the trading companies, New York banks no longer had total control of price manipulation because anyone could enter the futures market and get a better price. But this wasn't the case for long.

With the changes enacted by the Commodity Futures Trading Commission, especially the Commodity Act of 2000, banks were able to go overseas to trade unregulated commodities. Trading on these new electronic exchanges allowed banks to trade over the U.S. position limits because these markets are not regulated by the CFTC and the Securities and Exchange Commission. I personally believe this is what allowed U.S. banks to take crude oil prices to $147 a barrel in 2008. But this anomaly brought speculators into the marketplace who then used the crude oil futures at the New York Mercantile Exchange (NYME) to in effect break the cornering of crude oil by entering short sell positions.

By shorting the market, the speculators ultimately broke the market. This action lowered the crude market/price and made them the good guys for awhile. They stepped in before the government did and ideally, this is the way free enterprise should work. In other words, let the market do what the market's going to do. When the speculators took this step, they took crude oil down to the sixty dollar a barrel range which is the fair value area where the price remains today.

According to Platts in Singapore, the three largest crude oil traders in the world are first, Morgan Stanley; second, Goldman Sachs; third J. Aron and Company which is (surprise!) owned by Goldman Sachs. Given that information, shouldn't we all be asking 1) Why banks are the world's largest traders of crude oil? 2) Why prices got so distorted in 2008? And (3) most importantly, where is government intervention when it's needed? It's not like there isn't a precedent. In 1978 - 1980, the government intervened in the gold and silver markets, big time. The feds even acknowledged that the market had been cornered by large individual traders so why not acknowledge big banks? But this is only my opinion and what do I know? Well, I do know one thing, electronic trading has arrived and it is here to stay, so is the risk that comes with it, and that risk is getting bigger.

Back when bonds were in the small pit, there were a few companies and some large traders taking big risks. With the gigantic new pit, the number of large speculators and proprietary trading groups increased. Every brokerage house and investment bank set up trading operations as part of their customer business. In addition, many professional grain traders came to trade in these new and innovative markets. As a result, the new bond options pit became very busy and extremely crowded after the move to the new trading floor.

New traders entered the pit every day and one of them was Tom Baldwin. I'd heard that Tom won a trading contest in school and had decided to come and try his luck with the real deal. He bought a membership and started trading in the "Pit of Dreams" as so many called this new financial market. Tom's badge acronym was BAL and boy did he have them. He started trading ten lots, (a lot or contract was a $100,000 bond) so each transaction's value was one million dollars. Within a few months, he was trading one hundred lots and I was standing in front of him when Tom made his first thousand lot transaction. It blew everyone's mind, in fact, we didn't even have a hand signal for that quantity yet.

Hand signal or not, Tom was selling the market. He had previously sold one hundred lots at sixteen, then at seventeen, eighteen, nineteen, and finally one thousand lots at twenty to Jay Nolan, Goldman Sachs' broker. The pit went twenty-one bid for a moment and it was absolutely silent around Tom with every eye on him. We all knew that in a few seconds, he could lose his cute little ass. The duel was on.

Tom was down almost $75,000 since it's $31.25 a tick for one contract. That makes a thousand contracts $31,250 a tick. But the buyer panicked, started to sell, and the market caved in. The customer's broker offered nineteen, eighteen, then seventeen and still there were no trades. Tom finally bought one hundred at sixteen and he was in the money on his position. I pointed at his badge and said, "BAL stands for BALLS, not Baldwin." Tom laughed which broke the tension and got everyone back to trading. I grabbed a friend and left for coffee. Although I didn't stay for the end of the transaction, I think Tom made roughly $150,000 to $200,000 in just a few minutes. He would eventually become a multi-millionaire and a very well known trader - not just well known, but in my mind, a great trader because he had brass balls.

Occasionally, Tom and I would walk home together. He and his family lived in Sandburg Village, just two blocks from my place. While strolling down LaSalle Street one evening, we stopped across from the CBOT to admire a historic landmark called the Rookery Building. Built by Daniel Burnham in 1888, the Rookery has a magnificent lobby designed by Frank Lloyd Wright and is the oldest high rise still standing in Chicago. As we gazed at it, Tom said, "I think I'll buy this building someday. It's so elegant." Sure enough in 1989, through his Baldwin Development Inc., Tom became the owner of one of the city's most famous buildings, the Rookery.

Tom wasn't the only trader with a dream. That's why more and more people entered the pits, filling all the available new desk space as more and more member firms set up floor operations. That meant additional floor brokers were needed to fill customer orders. Dean Dziuba, my honey, had a big account that was moving to the pit's west end. I told him to stand next to Jay Nolan, the largest broker in the bond pit. Known as the million dollar broker, Jay filled orders for Goldman Sachs and most of the large firms.

But Dean had trouble taking my advice. Maybe it's because he was younger than me (yes, I was/am a cougar!). He was also one gorgeous stud muffin standing five feet , eleven inches tall with a large chest and shoulders to match, a small waist, brown hair, and a constant big smile with paralyzing blue-green eyes. But his most distinguishing feature was that he was crazy in love with me. Even so, this didn't keep Dean and I from arguing about Jay. Dean thought Jay wouldn't let him stand there and would push him out of the spot. But I knew better. After much prodding, Dean took his place near Jay and his back-up broker. I don't think I ever saw my stud muffin look so frightened. But Jay smiled at me across the pit and I smiled back. As I predicted, Dean got to stay. You see, I had an in with Jay. We bought our seats together and were among the first members to go into the financial pit. Jay had been my customers' gold broker and I had helped him become a floor broker back in 1977-78. Now, he did the same for Dean.

Soon, Dean got to fill some of Jay's overflow orders. At the time, the going floor broker rate was $1.50 per order and Dean proved to be a very good, very fast filling broker. In 1982 at age twenty-five, he was making thirty thousand dollars a month. Dean's big account flashed orders to him and sometimes their main broker, WIZ, would stand next to Dean in the pit and they would fill orders together.

Now with all this hard work, my stud muffin and I needed a vacation so we went to Jamaica. The day before we returned, WIZ put an ounce of cocaine in a glass of water and drank it. Immediately, he turned blue and died before the horrified eyes of my girlfriend Karen and her husband. Frantically, they called Chicago paramedics who tried to revive WIZ, but there was nothing to revive. His heart had burst and so did mine. You see, Dean and I were arguing constantly about drugs and WIZ's death didn't help. We broke up over it and immediately, Dean met someone else. Trading became very difficult for us both because I would see Dean everyday, all day, and his new girlfriend was in the visitor's gallery watching me. It was so upsetting that I stood and traded with tears running down my face. My friend HOG saw me and said, "Get out of here, Joyce." Then I really started to cry even though I was trying to keep quiet because people were watching. HOG, a big huge guy about 6'3", 280 pounds, picked me up, cuddled my face in his chest and carried me out of the pit. You see, when you pit trade, you stand in a big circle with 500+ people and everyone knows your business. It didn't help that I wore my heart on my sleeve and that heart was broken. So was I so I went home.

HOG was an Alpha man. Alpha was a small clearing house for member traders only. It was owned by Everett Clipp, an older, very experienced trader. Everett was a good friend of mine as were most of the guys who traded in the bond pit. A couple of us, Jim Zavesky, Jerry Veterick, Everett and I all had birthdays in the middle of October so every year, we had a big party. I think we had my annual twenty-fifth birthday party for about four years running. About five hundred male and twenty of us female traders attended the event. I was in charge of inviting the men and they were in charge of inviting the women. Funny how I got all the work again.

Anyway, the party was held at a pub around the corner from the Board of Trade. Everybody came and had a great drunken time. We started after the market closed at 2:30 PM and partied until we shut the place down. The Bondettes were all there and a few female runners too. One year, Everett was celebrating his sixtieth. We got a stripper to perform and she was the highlight of the event. I don't know where the guys found her, but she had an absolutely gorgeous body. Not a great face, but a great performer. (I'm embarrassed to say the guys called her "Bag lady" meaning she was so ugly you had to put a bag on her head to sleep with her.) But she was really a very nice girl. We invited her to stay and party in her black lingerie and she did. While she was enjoying herself, the guy who brought her left with the money and her coat but without her. In the meantime, we all took photos and I'm sure each of the five hundred male guests enjoyed the scene immensely. I know the situation sounds sexist, but the pit was - and is - such a pressure cooker that a party was the perfect chance to kick back and be normal friends and co-workers. With no competing for a tick, we could share a little fun for a little while.

A very little while because before you knew it, we were back in the pit the next day competing for trades, yelling, screaming, fighting, and calling each other dirty scum bags. The term meant a used rubber and I loved the phrase because it was SOOOO apropos. In this organized chaos, I sometimes stood next to Jim Bear. Jim was the father of quintuplet girls, the first ones born in the Chicago area. He was constantly warned by me not to get too close because I didn't want to catch anything from him like fertility. (Just kidding!) One day we were both trying to sell the market. Jim sold four contracts and gave me two. Just then the market hit buy stops and takes off like a bat out of hell on the up side. We had both sold the market and our short was getting killed - everyone was buying! We'd both lost so much money that we panicked. In our haste to get out we simultaneously bought our short positions in. I looked at him and said "Jim, we just bought the high of the day." We both put our hands up in the air, palms facing the pit and sold it at the high. The next second, the market crashed and we made back all the money we'd just lost. This up and down happens all day, everyday, and you share the yo-yo with your fellow traders. That day the down wasn't so bad because we both broke even. Still, Jim suggested we go out for coffee to recover and regain our rhythm, an invitation I gratefully accepted since the yo-yo sometimes made me fearful and nauseous. Unfortunately, it was a familiar feeling.

When I was in high school, a bunch of us were late going home and were running for the bus. As it pulled up to the corner and the first girl entered the street, she was hit by a speeding car as it illegally passed the stopped bus. She was thrown twenty-five, maybe thirty feet in the air, clear across the intersection. As her body coiled and jack-knifed, I thought she was dead. She landed in front of another oncoming car. Screaming, I ran to her, wanting to throw up. It felt like my stomach had fallen to my ovaries and then to my feet. I couldn't breathe. I've had the same feeling a few times in the pit. Granted, the pit is not life and death like that accident, but if you make an error or have a position on and take a big hit in the market, you virtually see your life flash before your eyes. This is the feeling of fear I've seen so many traders experience.

But Kenny Mitchell had a good piece of advice. Kenny was considered one of the best scalpers in the soybean pit (the other traders always know who the best trader is.) and we all watched and learned from him. One day he walked by and asked how things were going. I told him how dumb I was and that I was never going to do this stupid thing I'd done again. "Joyce, you'll do it again and again," Kenny responded, "it's the nature of the business." He was right, we all continued to make mistakes and lose money we shouldn't have because we got stubborn or momentarily lacked common sense.

This was also true when we fell in love and love was in the air. One of the larger filling brokers in the bond pit had decided to get married. He invited a group of us to go to his house for a celebration party and there were drinks, music, pizza and lots of laughs. As the evening progressed, much to my surprise and disgust, one of the Bondettes left the celebration with the host and headed for his bedroom. She returned about a half-hour later. I guess it was the last chance for romance but the next day the bloom was off the rose when the prospective groom bid fifteen to buy one hundred contracts and she sold them to him. Then he bid sixteen for another hundred and she said, "Sold!" She sold him another hundred at seventeen and now she was starting to lose big money. The whole pit went eighteen bid and he had one hundred to sell at that price, but instead of giving the trade to her, he gave it to his brother. She was bidding nineteen at the top of her lungs, paid twenty to get out of her position, and lost a lot of money. I wasn't sure how much, but later when I ran into her in the women's washroom I asked, "How much did he help you lose, about fifty thousand?" A lot more, she answered. I told her that if he'd done that to me he would be eating his teeth. He'd ignored certain pit courtesies and I was sure he would never have done that to a man but he was perfectly willing to do it to a woman. The bottom line was she'd screwed him the night before and he screwed her today in the pit. That's why you can't get involved with male traders. You are never going to be one of them so don't even try.

My colleague Michelle understood this or so I thought. She was trading big and making great money that she used to buy a terrific house in Old Town. We all thought her success was well deserved. Unfortunately, the pressure was getting to her and she'd started drinking Jack Daniels and popping pills. What she really needed was to walk away from trading for awhile. Eventually, she met a trader from the CME and got married. It was a lovely wedding and there were about ten or twelve of the Bondettes present. We got up to do a number with the band but singing wasn't our profession and it showed. Everybody was laughing hysterically as we wished Michelle and her new husband well. Soon Michelle sold her townhouse and bought a small farm with nice buildings and a pasture for her horse, an oasis, I thought. But the marriage didn't last and I heard rumors that he took half of everything she'd ever accumulated. After the divorce, Michelle tried to come back and trade but she never regained her rhythm or passion for our profession. Tall and slender with a beautiful face and red/blonde hair, she died early of – in my opinion – a broken heart.

And your heart really has to be in it if you're going to succeed in this business. I knew my own heart well and it wasn't in options even though I would occasionally take a position in the Bond Option pit. Like a lot of bond traders, my idea was to protect my bond futures position in options, but I just couldn't seem to make any money there. Then one day my bond chart looked really bullish so instead of risking a lot in bonds, I bought a couple of bond options instead. Now bond options are more complex than futures. As I studied my numbers, that is, the delta and gamma risk, I tried to decide which strike price I would open my position in.

As I anticipated, bonds were much higher the next day, so much higher that I would have made two thousand dollars per contract overnight in futures. By contrast, the option trade was a loser. How could that be? I was in the wrong strike price. Being no fool, I walked into the pit and asked, "what is the bid in the ninety call?" I was trading the ninety strike price. Nicely, one of the local traders informed me that the broker over there was ninety bid for one hundred contracts but everybody thought he had about five hundred total to buy. I said thank you, looked at the broker and offered to sell two. Everyone stared at me, wondering what I knew that they didn't. After all, I was experienced and from the big pit. That was all it took. Immediately, all the local traders sold to the buy order just like me and took out the five hundred contracts. The market fell sharply after I walked away. One by one the option traders strolled over to me and said "Thanks JOY."

What did I know? I knew I was right about the bonds going up. That's why I bought the bond options. Unfortunately, the specific option I bought didn't go up but everything else did. Bottom line, I was in the wrong strike price – the only one that didn't go higher so I had to give myself a GMO order also known as GIT ME OUT. While I was glad the other guys made money, I was really glad I didn't lose anymore. Ralph Goldenberg, my clearinghouse owner, said. "Before you bought the options did you ask the pit what strike price the bond traders were selling?" I was definitely in the option they were selling, but it's really hard to ask those questions when you're trading electronically. That very kind of situation is what's keeping the brick and mortar exchange floor open. Well, live and learn, I thought, and what I had learned was that options trading was not my game.

But the game itself was getting bigger all the time and we needed more room to play it. The Board of Trade bought the building across LaSalle Street and built another financial floor. The bond pit was enlarged and moved again. Eventually, this area also housed the CME Agriculture pits, Eurodollars and the Stock Index pits. CNBC televised its stock market, business and finance show from both exchange floors and onsite reporter Rick Santelli would have to run from the Mercantile Exchange to the Chicago Board of Trade to do his telecasts. I would occasionally bump into him on the street and we would walk together, discussing the news of the day and its impact on the markets. After the two exchanges merged, the CBOT became his permanent home. I knew Rick from the old days when he used to trade bonds. Now I get to see him on the floor or TV. I love his controversial coverage of the markets, his emphatic opinions on economic reports and the government's mishandling of the economy. His humorous rants and raves are watched throughout the world and like a typical trader, he always has a strong opinion, just like me.

Chapter Twelve

THE ECONOMIC INDICATORS AND REPORTS

It was one of those mornings when you wake up too early and your gut literally tells you it's not going to be a good day. Acid gurgled in the pit of my stomach, moving up my esophagus into my throat. I was tired and nauseous. To make matters worse, this particular week the markets were all over the place because interest rates and inflation were so volatile. In addition, the previous day's bond trading had been hyperactive with sporadic fast rallies and breaks in prices. Things were becoming more difficult with each passing hour. The risks were tremendous, people were edgy and cautious. Was it the flu or some bizarre virus? No, it was the impending release of the government's monthly Retail Sales report and possibly two to three additional reports as well. And "Reportiitis" wasn't the only "dis-ease" I risked catching.

The silence before the opening bell could be gut-wrenching. Sometimes traders are nervous and the pit has an obvious, almost contagious tension like a herd before it stampedes. Maybe the unspoken tension speaks volumes because the traders sure don't. In fact, it's so quiet you can hear a pin drop even though clerks are running orders into the pit while traders are hand signaling orders to their brokers and brokers' assistants are flashing price quotes to the trading desks. There is all this commotion without any sound. About thirty seconds before the opening bell, there's a low rumble - the beginning of verbal quotes starting to be heard - as brokers begin communicating bids and offers from the orders they've received. This is the market indication of the opening call and it helps establish the contract opening range. This in turn alerts traders and their customers to the market's direction and intensity - if they're paying attention - and I was because these figures are key if you're going to succeed.

And success was high on my priority list. That's why I'd put in years of study on these numbers. Unfortunately, many traders had no idea how to interpret them, in fact, they acted like the reports were a big mystery but the only mystery was why more people didn't make the effort to gain this knowledge. Compare that to something that was and is genuinely mysterious - knowing when the markets are about to change and when to buy and sell. This is all about instinct. In my case, feminine instinct. Bottom line, I often saw things others didn't, as Terry Cullerton found out.

Terry Cullerton, a fun Irishman, was a third generation CBOT trader and a large bond speculator. A bit on the heavy side with rich brown hair and eyes, Terry wore dark rimmed glasses. He had a very full face and was always smiling as he kidded around. Mainly a day trader, he scalped the market, entering and exiting quickly to make additional, small profits. On occasion, Terry would take large positions on the market direction. One morning, he came in long, He'd bought bonds the day before an important economic report was coming out. Personally, I didn't feel too good about the report and I saw Terry glance at me when it was released.

I hesitated, which meant the report didn't seem right. Then I searched for some type of revision and there it was on the Reuters board. Hesitation gone, my hands immediately went up in the sell position. I knew the traders would check Terry's, mine, and each other's reactions, looking to confirm the decision each was about to make. Talk about the quiet before the storm! Suddenly, traders and brokers started yelling, waving hands, pushing and shoving. The sound was deafening as clerks began screaming bids and offer quotes to the desks, then the desk clerks started yelling and bringing orders to their brokers or shouting "you're off!" - not the words you wanted to hear - especially Terry. He obviously had a large position so he panicked, rushing to get out. It was one of those life-flashing before your eyes moments. You could see it in Terry's face because the rumor was he'd lost $250,000 dollars in mere seconds. If you don't know the feeling - that sweaty trickle of fear down your back - you don't want to. Fortunately, years of experience have taught me not to break a sweat.

My fellow traders knew that a decade of handling huge customer accounts had made me really knowledgeable on economic indicators and I followed this information closely. I consistently used technical analysis to chart the market and had really great buy and sell points. That is, I regularly bought the lows and sold the highs. J.J. used to ask why I didn't trade larger and I said someday, when I was ready, I would. Unfortunately, poor Terry wasn't ready for anything except for the day to be over.

When the bell finally rang and the market closed, he looked terrible. I felt bad for him because I knew the figure was not going to be good and the market would break on the report as it flashed across from Reuters. Catching up with Terry at the end of the day, I said "Terry, I feel so upset about what happened to you today. I wish there was something I could do to make you feel better."

"Thanks JOY," he replied.

"Are you sure there's *nothing* I could do to make you feel better?" I purred in my best sexy, suggestive voice with a big smile on my face.

"Well maybe..." Terry, that crazy fun Irishman winked.

Then we both cracked up. Terry had been so depressed all day that our little therapy session made him laugh even harder. Here we were, the two of us, standing in the middle of the CBOT building lobby, laughing so hard tears were rolling down our cheeks and our stomachs ached. People walked by, knowing what had happened in the pit that day, and they probably thought Terry had lost his mind along with his money. Finally, he turned to me, tears streaming down his face.

"Joy, only you could make me laugh so hard on the worst day of my life. Thank you." Terry smiled as he said goodnight.

"See you tomorrow!" I called. The next morning we stood across from each other in the pit and I gave him the thumbs up sign as the bell rang. We had survived to trade another day.

Of course, it didn't always feel like we were surviving, sometimes it was more like the walking dead. There were mornings I would wake up depressed, then I'd say to myself "Rise and shine, you'll get them today!" And that was the attitude I had to take. You see when the bell rings, it's every trader for herself. Long ago, I'd realized that in the pits, like in life, the only person who could help me was me. And sometimes you have to help yourself grow thicker skin.

Before I started trading, I was full of fun. I only saw the JOY in life and was out partying all the time. But the reality of trading the markets, of living under their unforgiving ruthlessness, scares and changes you. To survive, much less thrive, my Pollyanna outlook had to go. I wasn't in Kansas anymore but I certainly didn't intend to be in the antechamber of hell either. Maybe Barbara Streisand said it best "What's too painful to remember we simply choose to forget. For it's the laughter we'll remember." That song best expresses my feelings about commodity trading. There were so many unforgettable, laughter filled moments that they wiped out the pain of a loss, a bad day, or even, the economic indicators and economic indicators could be painful. Very painful if you didn't know what to do with them. Fortunately, I did.

Economic indicators and their importance change year to year with world conditions. Back in the 70's and 80's, the Federal Reserve's Money Supply Report was the big deal. Every Thursday after the market closed, the M1 and M2 figures would be released at precisely 3:30 PM, Central Standard Time. M1 represents currency in circulation, travelers checks, demand deposits, and checking accounts. M2 includes M1 plus a broader range of information such as economic indicators of inflation, savings accounts, time deposits and balances in retail money market mutual funds. These figures represented inflation and the up/down movements of interest rates – and they had a dramatic impact on the bond market. Did I say dramatic? I mean catastrophic.

The morning after this money supply data was released could be an absolute blood bath for many traders. Going home long or short on Thursday night was a big speculative trade. That meant every Friday morning, the opening would be erratic and chaotic because everybody was responding to the money supply figure with some traders trying to liquidate their open positions before the weekend. Amazingly, the markets no longer give this report the time of day. But they still snap to attention when it comes to the Federal Reserve.

The monthly Federal Reserve Meetings can cause the markets to be very skittish. There were times when it seemed like the Fed was raising or lowering interest rates every week. They would do it by buying or selling overnight repos or doing customer overnight repos or reverse overnight repos. Now "repos" is a form of short-term borrowing that the Federal Reserve uses to make collateralized loans to primary dealers. A repo temporarily adds reserve balances to the banking system. This is usually done on an overnight basis and they offset the transactions the following day. In a reverse repo, the Fed temporarily drains balances from the banking system. Dealers offer interest rates at which they lend money to the Federal Reserve versus the Fed's general collateral - usually Treasury Bills. These operations have a short-term, self-reversing effect on bank reserves. There were times when the Fed entered the market almost everyday at 10:30 AM to do this. Generally, the market would ease down before their intervention and take off after the repos. For awhile I made good money playing this game because I remembered that old saying "Buy the rumor, sell the fact."

And the fact was that I needed to broaden my horizons. One way I did that was by serving on several CBOT committees. I was elected to the Chicago Board of Trade Associate Members Committee; was Director of the CBOT Educational Research Foundation; a Member of the CBOT Marketing and Education Committee; and a Member of the CBOT Floor Conduct Committee. What I loved about this last one was that when I yelled, guards came running. Then the day finally came when I was running - OUT OF STEAM!

It was 1984 and I'd been trading bonds for 7 1/2 years. I started to have burn out and trading bonds had become rough, very rough. It was difficult to make money because my heart wasn't in it anymore. My concentration was slipping and my timing was off. This wasn't uncommon. You see, traders are like athletes. We go through streaks when we can't do anything wrong and at other times we can't do anything right. One evening after work, Billy O'Connor and I were talking about my increasingly difficult relationship with trading. Billy knew that at that moment, I hated my world. A few days after this conversation, he came down to the floor and motioned me out of the pit. He asked if I'd meet with him and his brother Eddie after the close. They had a proposition for me. "Sure," I said. Little did I know it was the proposition of a lifetime.

Chapter Thirteen

THE MMI PIT

Eddie, Billy, and I met in their private offices at O'Connor and Company in the Chicago Board of Trade Building. They were on one of the top floors with a beautiful view of the city and Grant Park. Complete with a large fireplace and balcony, it was almost like a penthouse apartment and during the summer months, their secretaries would go out onto the balcony to sunbathe. Amidst this stunning setting, Eddie told me a stunning piece of news. He said a new pit was about to open at CBOT and they intended to be participants big participants.

It was the MMI, the American Stock Exchange's Major Market Index, designed to measure the performance of the top twenty blue chip stocks and very similar to the Dow Jones Industrial Average (DJIA). In fact, 19 of the MMI's 20 stocks were listed on the DJIA. Developed in 1983 by the American Stock Exchange (ASE), the MMI would open for trading at CBOT in summer, 1984.

The O'Connor's needed a Floor Broker - the person who fills customer orders in the pit - and they needed someone they could trust. Someone with enough experience to oversee a lot of new people just entering the business. Someone like me. YIPPEE! A stock index at the CBOT was the exchange's entry into equity futures and the financial community was waiting with baited breath to see how it worked. Several of O'Connor's grain traders were very interested in trading this new index and making markets. They had a small group of in-house traders called the Smith Brothers who would be using the index for arbitrage against the Chicago Board Options Exchange (CBOE) OEX, the option index contract on 100 listed stocks and against the Chicago Mercantile Exchange (CME) Standard & Poors' (S&P) 500 stock index.

To further these goals, the O'Connor's had recently opened a new, proprietary trading company called O'Connor & Associates. O'Connor & Associates was a private group trading only for itself, as compared to O'Connor and Company which was a trading/brokerage house for member traders to clear their/their customers trades. O'Connor & Associates would be trading baskets of stocks, that is, 100 shares each of 30 DJIA listed stocks vs the S&P Options, MMI, and the CBOE OEX options. If they liked my work, I could potentially pick up some or all of the O'Connor & Associates arbitrage business because they were going through the O'Connor desk where I'd be stationed. If I could make this happen, I would earn an excellent living, but all the errors would be mine because I would be an independent broker working for myself. Can you say pressure? But it was also opportunity. Big opportunity.

The O'Connor's knew I had done some customer brokerage order filling in my career, but not a lot. Even so, they were willing to take a chance on me, saying I would learn as business picked up. They also told me not to worry. Their main concern was having someone honest who they knew they could trust. "Send me your best looking, most experienced stud muffin from the CME S&P pit for my clerk and we have a deal!" I said. And what a deal it was. I basically agreed to leave the large bond pit for one year and start another new market.

Then Billy and I headed down to the old Bond Room to choose where the trading desk would be. I WAS SO EXCITED - AND I WAS HOME because this very spot was where I'd spent five years of my career. Billy thought the curve of the pit would be a good place for the desk but I said, "No way." The ceiling at that end of the room was all steel beams with metal overlay. I could practically hear the sound of voices reverberating horribly at that end of the pit and I knew what I was talking about - literally. I had experienced the racket first hand as a bond trader and remember how my own high pitched voice could even set the glass wall to shaking. When I told Billy this, he laughed.

"Joyce," he chuckled, "look how your experience is helping already."

Finally, we decided on a prime location. The center of the room was the lead option spot (the most active trading month) and our desk would be placed right there. Would we have any trouble getting permission for all this? No. You see the exchange did whatever Billy wanted because he was about to become the next Chairman of the Chicago Board of Trade.

A few weeks after this discussion, Terry Biondo arrived from the CME to work with me. He was about twenty years old with blonde hair and an Italian Stallion body. A fantastic body. In addition, he was an experienced Arb clerk and to sweeten the bargain, he had great hand signals. Terry had to take a lot of kidding because now he reported to a woman - me. The terrific thing was that I really liked him and the feeling was mutual. Bottom line, we worked very well together. He was a terrific support now that I was on the top step, center stage, and had literally become Joyce, Queen of the Mountain. Billy and Eddie were happy and I was definitely enjoying the change.

Terry's great hands (signals, that is) were extremely important. Back in the 1940's when an open out-cry trade was completed inside the pit, the transaction was considered a gentleman's agreement and the buyer and seller would shake hands upon completion. As the pits became busier and more crowded, the trade procedure changed and upon completion you made physical contact by tapping the other trader's shoulder or body. As the pits became more chaotic and crowded still, it became impossible for traders to walk through the wall of flesh and have this key physical contact to seal the deal. Instead, a chopping hand signal was devised using the wrist motion of a handshake. This replaced physically touching the other trader. The chopping motion meant "sold" and now you hear traders say the word "Sold" accompanied by this chop of the hand. Eventually, the hand chop movement alone became the signal from the broker to the trading desk that their order had been filled.

Hand signals like the chop were essential in the new, larger pits. For example, a big portion of the trades in today's markets might be part of a spread or arbitrage transaction where speed is extremely important. The customers could be trading at two different exchanges and if the broker can't get the trade filled at a specific price or the other exchange has moved ahead, our price on the order would immediately be canceled or changed. The signal for cancel is loudly shouting the words "you're off!" The corresponding hand signal is a slashing movement with the fingers moving left to right across the throat as in off with your head! The reverse of the slash sign with fingers toward the pit moving left to right is a market order. Buying is always hands toward your body and selling is always away from you with hands out facing the pit. Fingers to the forehead represents ten to ninety-nine contracts. One finger pointed to the forehead with the slash fingers out means Buy 10 contracts at the market. One to nine contracts is represented by fingers to the chin. There. You're now ready to trade. Easy, right ?

And is it very easy to make money trading. The problem is that it's also easy to lose money – maybe easier – as many people found out.

Chapter Fourteen

JAMES RITCHIE

Just as trading is feast or famine, the trading day alternates between busy and boring. One day there was a rare lull in the chaos. I was relaxing, but behind me sensed the presence of a tall structure. A very tall structure. Since only my clerk with his top step badge was allowed to stand in this spot, I turned to see who was there. Behind me was an overpowering, handsome man. So overpowering and handsome that I was actually speechless for a second – something rare for me. I smiled. "Hi handsome," I said, regaining my voice, then I moved to the left so he could enter the pit.

"Who is this breathtaking guy with the unbelievable blue eyes?" I asked myself. Those eyes looked soft and gentle, but I suspected they could turn black and cold as steel, put chills up your spine or bring you down to your knees. I watched Blue Eyes make a trade and waited anxiously to hear what he said. By then the whole pit was whispering his name, Jim Ritchie, Jim Ritchie, Jim Ritchie. He turned around, came up the step and again I stepped aside with a smile on my face. Jim's mouth didn't smile back but his eyes sure did and right at me. WOW! It was the highlight of my day, my week, maybe even my life.

Joe and James Ritchie owned Chicago Research and Trading Co. (CRT). CRT was one of the first organizations to computerize theoretical option valuations. They were a proprietary trading firm like O'Connor & Associates and both companies were spearheading a new way of trading. CRT's floor broker stood to my right and when

Jim entered the pit to make a small trade he stood in front of his floor trader, right by me.

CRT started program trading in the early 1980's and it went well, very well, From 1983 to 1993, they grew to 700 employees and eventually, the company was sold to

NationsBank for about $225 million. O'Connor & Associates followed suit, eventually selling for $300 million.

Years later I read about the O'Connor sale and said to Billy "Why didn't you tell me you were worth that much money? I would have chased your ass to the end of the world."

"Sure, Joyce," Billy laughed, "but don't believe everything you read in a book."

Billy and Eddie came from an average, middle-class Irish family. Likewise, Joe and James Ritchie also came from an average, middle class family as do many people at the exchanges. In addition, many are second or third generation traders. Contrary to popular myth, it wasn't a world of the lazy or rich and famous, but a universe of intelligent, educated, aggressive go-getters. And I wanted to go for him every time Jim Ritchie entered the pit.

A week later I had my chance. Once again I said "Hi handsome." Jim looked deep into my eyes and gave me a slight nod of acknowledgement. Then he stepped into the pit to make a trade and left. A few days later, business in the pit began to pick up and we were busy. I'd just completed a sale of 100 MMI's and I sensed someone coming up behind me. You develop this sixth sense after spending time on the trading floor. Your eyes and ears have to quickly grasp the tone of the markets and the emotional state of the traders around you. As Jim walked up and said "Hi Joy," the sound of his voice actually stopped trading for a second. You see, no one had ever heard him speak. We weren't even sure he had a voice! But he did, especially when he looked at me and gave a slight smile with those penetrating eyes.

You're probably wondering why I made such a big deal over Jim Ritchie's eyes. Well, my mother once told me "your eyes are the windows to your soul." I didn't know Jim Ritchie that well, in fact, I only saw him a few times, but I could see what my mother said was true. In fact, he had eyes like mine. Eyes that showed no fear. Fifteen years later I would have even more evidence of this.

You see, when Joe and Jim Ritchie were very young, they lived in Afghanistan. Joe was ten and Jim was just a few months old. Their father was a civil engineer and their mother a teacher, living in Kabul on a four year humanitarian mission.

Their experience and love for the people stayed with them, so much so that the Ritchies personally backed a pre-9/11 plan to overthrow the Taliban. They did this via their friendship with the freedom fighter Abdul Haq. Haq had allied the regional tribal chiefs from southern and eastern Afghanistan, then tried to forge a national coalition by uniting with the Northern Alliance. The goal was to create a nationwide force to fight Bin Laden and the Taliban - the same Bin Laden and the same Taliban that the U.S. originally backed in the war against the invading Soviet Army.

For three years, the Ritchies had tried to get Washington to focus on the Afghan situation. Then came the 9/11 attack on the World Trade Center and everything changed. The Ritchies probably saw it coming. You, see in early October, 2001, Jim Ritchie entered Pakistan with a fortune he planned to use to unite and fund the Northern Alliances. He was at a hotel with Haq intending to leave at five the next morning to enter Afghanistan. But Haq departed at four, leaving Jim behind. A blessing, since Abdul Haq and his men would be captured enroute, tortured and killed by Taliban fighters on October 25, 2001. Thanks to Haq, Jim Ritchie's life was spared so he and Joe could continue their efforts.

Carol Marin, a reporter with CBS-TV Chicago, hosted a special about the Ritchies on 60 Minutes II. It was called Fighting the Taliban. Filmed in Afghanistan, it ran on American television during the month of December, 2001. I called every woman I knew and told them to catch the show. I said, "James Ritchie is the best looking rich guy I know and you have to see him." There was a method to my seemingly superficial madness. This was my way of getting people to watch the interview and listen to what was really going on in Afghanistan. Those Afghani women live a life of slavery and violence and I had been following their plight for quite some time. As the show went on, my phone rang off the hook and these conversations continued as the U.S. declared a war on terror.

Just as the war on terror continues today, Joe and James Ritchie are still doing their part, actively working to help the oppressed people of Afghanistan and other countries around the world. I'm proud to know them and say we not only stood together at the Board of Trade, but stand together for what is right, in the pits and out.

Chapter Fifteen

THE SMITH BROTHERS

A short time after the IMM opened the Smith Brothers arrived, or maybe I should say the "O'Smith" Brothers since my colleagues were Irishmen. Jerry and Jim were fraternal twins from a family of eleven children. At 6'3", Jerry was big, husky, and over two hundred pounds. A unique, totally amazing man, he had brown hair with red highlights that glimmered in the sun and accented his piercing green eyes. By contrast, Jimmy's eyes were steel blue. He had coal black hair and a smallish, 5'7" frame. When they stood together, they looked like father and son. People didn't even know they were twins until you pointed it out. Then you realized they looked alike but had totally different personalities.

Jerry worked with me on the Board of Trade floor and Jimmy worked at the Chicago Board Options Exchange OEX pit. A third brother, Bobby, was at the Chicago Mercantile Exchange in the S&P pit. They arbitraged the three markets buying and selling one against the other.

Jerry was brilliant in a sometimes distant kind of way. One day he was looking at me as I signaled that the market was 5 bid at 6. He gave me an order to buy ten contracts at five. Without moving, I immediately signaled "filled." Then Jerry told one of the guys to sell at the market on the other exchange. But within a second, the market fell and instead of buying ten at five, I bought ten at four, a much better price. We were already filled on the sale at the high when Jerry came running over to the pit and said, "What the hell did you see that told you the market would tank?" I smiled. Jerry was always asking me this question and I always gave him the same answer - women's intuition. And that was the truth. Sometimes I could see or feel things other people didn't and this was typical for me. You see, when you're an arb broker, you're supposed to move fast and be accurate. You're not suppose to think, you're supposed to know. And one thing I knew was that Jerry and I would be really good friends.

We would meet at the Sign of the Trader bar on the first floor of the Board of Trade building for lunch or a cocktail with Billy O'Connor. All my girlfriends had crushes on Jerry and with good reason. He was good looking, cultured and bright, a very caring man.

One day, I introduced Jerry to my Irish girlfriend, Tara Murphy. Tara had just moved to Chicago from the Virginia/Washington, D.C. area. She was a bigwig at the Federal Reserve and within two months, had closed down a couple of my favorite institutions - Continental Bank and United of America Bank. Tara clarified some of the confusion around the closures in the Fed's press release, telling anxious customers "don't worry, I have a buyer and everything is fine." What put those two storied institutions under? I can't speak for United of America, but Continental's demise can be summed up in ten words: William "Billy" O'Connor, Chairman of the Chicago Board of Trade - AKA my friend and business associate. It seems Billy had moved all of the Exchange's Customer Segregated money from Continental Bank to Harris Bank. Continental couldn't open the next day because it didn't have enough cash on hand in deposits and had to seek Federal Reserve protection. Billy told me "there were rumors flying all over Europe that morning that Continental Bank was having serious financial troubles." So to protect the CBOT, Billy moved the Customer Segregated funds to a more stable bank. It was a difficult, highly courageous move for him because the CBOT and Continental Bank had, until then, had a long, successful relationship. But Billy put himself on the line for the Exchange's well-being and to keep our customers' money safe. Talk about guts, not to mention ethics. I was proud to be working with him.

Likewise, ethics were why Tara, Jerry, and I were extremely respectful of each other's business privacy and confidentiality agreements we had to be, we also wanted to, because we were professionals. Even so, we shared a lot, So much so, that Tara developed a real attraction to Jerry. Unfortunately, she could never get anything more than a friendship going with him. Years later, Jerry said, "I had no idea she was interested in me, if I did, I would've married her." Like I said, Jerry was so brilliant he could sometimes miss the obvious.

What was obvious to all of us was that the brothers were doing well in a really difficult market. Much of that was because of Jerry. If he wasn't on the floor, he was always on the computer. Jerry had devised a system that could keep your option positions consistently Delta Neutral. He called it "The Modifier" and it went way beyond "what if" testing software. You see, the Modifier was constructed around an advanced mathematical algorithm. The algorithm was designed to find solutions that modified an existing options portfolio's risk profile so that profile matched the desired risk parameters. It was intended for trading groups with large options positions when those groups had to quickly fine tune risk parameters including the portfolio's "greeks" - its delta, gamma, and theta exposure in a real time trading environment. Delta represents a position's total market risk, gamma its volatility risk, and theta its duration profitability. The algorithm was a work of genius, but even geniuses get tired and I had begun to wonder if the financial world was getting to Jerry.

He had taken a couple of weeks off when I ran into him at the bus stop across from the Board of Trade. He said, "I need to talk to you. Let's have lunch together tomorrow." To say I was curious was an understatement. The Smith brothers had been trading with me for about two years now and I knew them fairly well. But when we met at the Sign of the Trader, Jerry seemed different. I couldn't quite put my finger on it. Traders lost money one day and made money the next. You got used to people being moody and quiet - it was part of the game. But Jerry never said anything when he suffered a loss. He was very private about their trading so I wasn't sure if that's what was on his mind, but I can tell you he BLEW MY MIND when he finally shared.

You see, Jerry had decided to change his life - not just change it, but turn it upside down. He announced that he was going to enter the seminary and become a Catholic priest. Of course, I was shocked! He started his studies at age thirty-one and six years later was ordained Father Jerome Smith. While he was away, Jerry and I stayed in touch. During this same time, Jimmy got married and had eight children. A few years later, Bobby got married too, moving to Elmhurst near my nephew. He and Jimmy are still trading today while Jerry trades in a different commodity - souls.

Which only goes to show how many different people you meet in the markets, and how many are good guys like the Smith Brothers and Billy and Eddie O'Connor.

Chapter Sixteen

O'CONNOR & ASSOCIATES

While filling orders for member traders at O'Connor and Company, I would occasionally get big orders from O'Connor & Associates in Chicago and New York which was great. Things were going well, very well. The MMI was doing roughly 28,000 to 30,000 contracts a day. It was good volume although not nearly as much as the S&P pit over at the CME. But it was getting easier to fill orders with more liquidity in the pit and we were getting lots of new, local traders. For the most part, these were scalpers and day traders who were in and out of the markets quickly. These types of traders tighten up bid and offers, creating liquidity that in turn draws in position traders. Bottom line, the MMI was a fast-paced market and it could get dangerous. Fortunately, so could I.

O'Connor & Associates was starting to use me more and more. Randy was their main floor trader and I felt he trusted and liked working with me. Randy had beautiful, reddish blonde hair, a stocky build, and was at that oh-so-critically necessary height for a man: six feet tall. He also had a cute personality and was usually smiling - all in all - a really nice guy. I would get a lot of unusual orders from Randy/ O'Connor & Associates like "in the next three minutes you can sell five hundred contracts." If I got them filled right way, they would give me another five hundred to sell. If I didn't sell all of the order they would cancel the balance. Everything was verbal with a clerk watching closely, ready to yell "You're off!"

To make matters even more complicated, the exchange was changing the price structure of the MMI contract. That meant we were running two pits side by side. These pits traded simultaneously to allow existing customers to roll into the new contract. Randy was in one pit and I was in the other and he would signal me or verbally tell me what to do. It was chaotic, dangerous and the brokers were tense and a little feisty because the risk of making an error was high

But Randy was a great customer and I was making good money with him. Unfortunately, this caused some "broker envy" which I realized when another filling broker tried to sabotage my relationship with O'Connor & Associates. I had just completed a trade with this guy then turned to confirm it with Randy when suddenly the broker purposely lies and says he did not make that trade with me - even though he saw me confirm it. I screamed at the %^&(*& "I was your first ten lot on the sixty lot order!" Then I walked over to Randy and informed him that the broker broke the trade. Randy just smiled. "I saw what happened. It's okay Joyce, don't worry."

I was still pissed and glaring at the guy when what I'll call "market justice" (or maybe the goddess Ceres atop the CBOT Building!) set in. You see, the market suddenly moved in Randy's direction and he took profits immediately. About ten minutes later, Randy walked over and said, "I'm done for the day. We made ten thousand dollars on that error trade. Nice job, Joyce." The broker who tried to screw me heard it all, but all I heard was the news that I was now O'Connor & Associates' main arbitrage broker. It was a great opportunity that came with great risk.

You see, because of the speed and changing markets, filling orders gets dangerous, especially during busy moments when you might miscount or when the market price gets away from you. If an independent broker like me confirms a wrong price or quantity, she is held to that fill. This means I have to guarantee the fill and make up any differences in price and volume. These miss fills are called errors or out-trades and it was my responsibility to see that such problems did not occur. In other words, I wanted to be sure trades went to the customer at the right price and quantity.

One day, O'Connor & Associates was a heavy seller of the market. They signaled me to sell one hundred at five and when I filled that order, they signaled me to sell another one hundred, also at five. Sometimes this would continue until we sold a total of nine hundred contracts. After about five of these fast, sequential orders, there was mass confusion in the pit as it absorbed the quantity of my selling and sought a sort of equilibrium. I was trying to straighten out how many contracts a new local wanted to purchase, but he confused me and for just a second, I lost count. At that exact moment, a broker offered to buy the balance of the order. I told him "forty-six." But I was wrong. I actually needed to sell sixty so I was missing fourteen fills. My ARB clerk heard what sounded like a completion of the trade and told the customer he was filled. Then the clerk shoots me another order to sell one hundred at five. It was getting thin and the market was starting to move lower, but luck was with me and I was able to sell one hundred fourteen at five. TALK ABOUT SAVING MY BOOTY FROM A BIG ERROR AND A FINANCIAL LOSS! WHEW!

But I barely had time to absorb this when the next order came to sell one hundred at four, then one hundred at three, with about twenty or thirty orders in quick succession after that. The market was falling fast and O'Connor was selling everything it could. My clerk actually had to send a couple of orders to another broker who was then competing with me which increased the tension a hundred-fold. At the end of the day, the market collapsed but I was still standing - barely. In just a few minutes that fourteen lot error would've cost me about ten thousand dollars. I don't know how I got my composure back so fast after my mistake but I did. Ultimately, the only money I lost was the three hundred dollars in brokerage commission that I didn't receive for the two orders that went to the backup broker. But that loss wasn't really a loss at all - it was the small price I paid for an amazing lesson in resiliency and staying calm and focused, grounded in my professional experience.

Chapter Seventeen

IN THE PITS

A new local named Don Sliter appeared in the MMI pit. He'd been a clerk for Henry Shatkin, a big trader in grains, and had recently decided to try his luck trading for himself. At the time, bonds were trading at 500,000 to 750,000 contracts a day while other areas were trading a fraction of that. The Bondettes used to ask me how things were going in the (meow!) "little" MMI pit. Laughing, I would answer, "Bonds, who cares about bonds, you've got to see Sliter, the new guy. He wears his corduroy jeans way too tight and has a lot of love to give." One by one, the Bondettes cruised the MMI pit to check him out.

Sliter was a former southpaw baseball pitcher and this time around, he was on the mound longer than he was in the pit. The reason? Sliter took a big hit in the market and had to pay money back to Shatkin to cover his losses. He returned to being a clerk which must have been difficult for him given that everybody on the floor knew what had happened. Sliter also worked late doing out-trades. I was impressed. Where the Bondettes saw a struggling guy in tight jeans, I saw someone with enough drive and determination to start all over again. The kind of guy who holds his head high. I knew that someday Sliter would walk back into the pit and start all over again, this time with a different result.

And I was right. In a couple of months, Sliter was back trading bigger than ever, intent on catching his dream. I used to kid him and tell him to cut back his trading size, but Sliter kept doing it his way.

Eventually, he got his rhythm and left us to go to the CME S&P pit. By the time I went back to the Merc a few yeas later, he'd became one of the richest local traders there.

Because we were overcrowded and needed more space, the MMI pit was moved into the old silver pit located in the main grain room. (The silver market had gotten very quiet and we didn't need as much room as we did in the Hunt brother's days.) It was then that I started receiving small orders from traders in the corn pit. One day when their clerk ran the orders over to me I asked him, "why am I getting these?" Grinning, he explained, "your high pitched voice hits the center of the grain room ceiling and reflects into the center of the corn pit as if you're standing right there. Since we can hear you so well, we want you to fill the orders because we can tell immediately when you've filled the trade."

I must admit that my professional order filling voice was more like a scream, and this was an absolutely necessary job skill. Like on the day a broker in the MMI pit traded under my bid. I started screaming "I am five bid, you idiot, get that four trade out. You can't trade under the existing bid."

"I didn't hear you!" he said, whereupon the whole pit started laughing, including me. If the distant corn pit could hear me, I was pretty sure this guy a few inches away could. In fact, everybody could hear me, that's why they had to refit the center of the four story ceiling to absorb my high pitched voice so it didn't reverberate all over the room.

I wish I could tell you that I sometimes lowered my voice and was Ms. Sweetness and Light, but that's not the way it was in the pit. On good days I screamed. On bad days I screamed, cried, and maybe had to belt someone. It was a cut throat world. I fought for my spot everyday because the broker next to me was constantly trying to get my accounts but it didn't work. I was Joyce, Queen of the Mountain.

Once, I received an order to sell two contracts. Everyone wanted to buy so I hit the first two guys bidding because you can only split a two lot order one way. That's right. One and one equals two. But a broker started yelling at me, "YOU RE THE WORST, YOU'RE THE WORST!"

I wasn't in the mood to fool with him. I threw open my trading jacket, pushed my breasts out, and ran my fingers through my hair. "That's not what my date last night said." But instead of being charmed by my joke, he went absolutely nuts screaming and shouting that we should take this into the alley. The alley? "Excuse me," I arched an eyebrow, "but you are not man enough to take me out in the alley." Besides, the days of fistfights in the alley were long gone - except, apparently, for this jerk because he starts screaming, "GUYS, HOLD ME BACK, HOLD ME BACK!" He looked and sounded so idiotic that no one moved or tried to stop him. After all, what was this maniac going to do? Hit a petite, one hundred ten pound girl? Not to mention that my little stud muffin, Dean, was standing between us right in the center of the pit. Realizing he had no support, Mr. Jerk-face backed down. You see, the guys had learned early on that if you pick on JOY, you'll regret it - unless you want to look like a total moron - so everyone left me alone. It was all part of my verbal protocol in the pit, and while I'm at it, let me say a word about the verbal "protocol" of sexual harassment. I'm the first to admit I enjoyed sexually harassing the men, but only if THEY STARTED IT FIRST - which they often did. It was really a form of relief. Filling brokerage wasn't - isn't - the easiest job and you take a lot of verbal abuse throughout the day. Being a local wasn't easy either but that's a different kind of pressure.

I tried to keep this in mind whenever another new broker entered the pit. The appearance of an unknown on the scene was part of all the fun and excitement like a daily shoot out at the O.K. Corral. I remember the time a young, inexperienced guy working for a large commission house walked into the pit. Occasionally, he would fill small orders. One day, he had an order to sell a thirty lot at seven. He was standing next to me holding the order in his hand. Luckily, I saw what the order said, "Sell thirty MMI at seven." The market went six bid at seven offer. He said nothing. That was a big mistake because he should have put both hands in the air facing the pit and offered to sell thirty at seven. All of sudden, the pit went seven bid traded eight, eight bid.

Now, this kid owed his customer a fill - he was liable and HE FROZE! With my left hand I grabbed the order and with my right fist, punched him dead center in the chest, knocking him out of the pit. I handed the order to his regular filling broker (the guy who wanted to take me in the alley) and luckily, the broker filled the order at seven because in just three seconds, the market was back trading at five. The youngster was actually leaning over the desk dry heaving. Missing the order had scared him to death. I saw it clear as day, the kid's first big experience with life passing before his eyes. I was afraid he was going to throw up and I backed away since I had on a nice St. John knit pants outfit. When he finally recouped about a half-hour later, he came back in the pit and softly whispered, "Thanks, JOY."

And it was my pleasure.

Chapter Eighteen

BLACK MONDAY

The week before Black Monday, the stock market was getting very skittish, traders were nervous, and the market had become extremely thin. A buy or sell order would move the market up or down more than it should have. It was almost like a premonition.

Standing one step down from me, almost in my face, was John McGuire. He stood 6'6" and weighed a solid two hundred and forty pounds. John had played on the Chicago Bears' taxi squad for awhile and then became a grain trader at the CBOT. I'd known him for many years and we had been neighbors in Aspen, Colorado, where we both lived for a short time. John owned a bar there and partied too much while I was running away from a bad romantic break-up so we were friends, not lovers- but that was friends with a capital "F".

When John was in the pit, no one with a brain yelled at me, even when he was wearing a cast from his ankle to his hip due to a horse riding accident. One day, the Chicago Research and Trading Co. broker and I had a quantity difference on an order and it cost me thirty-eight hundred dollars. Adding to that, the guy starts screaming at me in the pit after the market opens. Turning to him, John said, "you don't talk that way to her," then my protector charged at the guy. Everyone dived out of John's way as he stormed down the steps with his cast making a loud banging noise as it hit the stairs. "Wait!" I called to John, "the jerk is only 5'6", barely comes up to your belt buckle and is a waste of your time and energy." The broker sure didn't like the sound of that, but he knew I'd saved his ass. John came to a halt, "you're right, JOY, he's NOT worth my time and energy." Then John yelled, "You little creep, don't you ever talk to her that way again." The broker took a deep breath, said O.K., and mumbled some contrite words in my direction. He didn't say so, but he was thrilled I had saved him from certain death-by-John.

But this broker wasn't the only one with a short fuse. Tempers were getting hot because the market was unusually thin and rough to trade. It was like that old saying, "damned if you do or damned if you don't." My fellow traders and I couldn't make money if we bought or sold - always a very bad sign. The charts looked even worse and the feeling in the pit was scary. Very scary.

The next day, Wednesday, October 14, I bought one MMI contract from John that turned out to be the high of the day. Instantly, I received an order to sell one at the market. John was bidding for one so I sold to him. Then I said, "Lunch is on me today. You eat and go home because it's getting too thin to continue trading." And I was right. The market got thinner and thinner, crashing 130 points from the high which in those days was a big drop. Now two things made the market go down - heavy selling and a lack of buying - an ominous pattern.

The next morning, I came in and had one out-trade with John, buying the high of the day from him. When I found his out trade clerk, I asked where John was since I hadn't seen him around. The market was opening in twenty minutes and the call was 100 lower. I had to get into the pit and his clerk had no idea of John's whereabouts. I figured he must have gone home with a card in his pocket so I told her to "card the trade for him." She said she couldnít do that without his okay. I told her to look at the close and card the trade at this price which was the previous day's high. She looked at the board and saw that the price was 150 points above the close. "Really," I assured her, "it's a good trade." Quickly, she carded the trade for him. "If John doesn't arrive by the opening," I continued, "put an order in for him to buy the position back at the market on the opening. Then, give the order to any broker but me," I said since I knew I would be busy on the opening.

Three minutes before the opening bell, John walked onto the floor, card in hand, ready to trade. "What should I do?" he asked me. "Get out, get out right away!" I shouted, "never kick a gift horse in the mouth." At that moment, the market opened ninety dollars lower. John made about eight thousand dollars on a one lot. This was my second problem of the week. Now I had two large out-trades. What was going on? I didn't make errors, at least not errors of this magnitude, but I was getting very nervous and so was the market. It was Thursday, October 15, 1987, my annual twenty-fifth birthday party. I was all dressed up and ready to celebrate after the close. Instead, I had one drink with the guys at the Sign and headed home. Before I left, I called my mom and told her and dad to come and meet me. With that feminine intuition which I'd inherited she knew something was up and agreed that they would come right away. I think mom could sense the danger surrounding my scary, risky, erratic life in the pits. Somehow she knew I'd become terrified of the markets -probably before I admitted it to myself. And now I had to face the question I'd been avoiding - WHAT HAD HAPPENED TO MY LACK OF FEAR?

Needing some time alone to think before they arrived, I decided to walk home and reflect on my life. It was a beautiful, sunny day in Chicago, so I strolled down Michigan Avenue past all the great stores. Right in front of the John Hancock Building, one of the tallest condominium structures in the world, I ran into John McGuire. Albeit with a limp, he was proudly high stepping down the street. Under his arm was a brand new black Gucci horse crop. Seeing me, John couldn't wait to show me his purchase and tell me it came with a matching Ralph Lauren saddle. I could just picture him riding his Irish Philly with that saddle on her back. Smiling I said, "see you tomorrow" as he headed west and I continued walking north toward my condo on Lake Shore Drive.

I had a wonderful birthday dinner with my parents. Then I told them that after much thought and consideration, I was going to retire from pit trading tomorrow. As always, mom and dad were 100% behind me and they agreed that maybe it was time to stop for awhile. I walked into work on Friday, October 16, 1987, and carefully checked all my trades to be sure I had no out-trades or errors and that I was flat with no positions. Then I left the floor and went up to see Billy O'Connor.

Luckily, Billy hadn't left for the trading floor and was still in his office. Walking in, I informed him that I was retiring from filling orders. When I took the job, I had committed to one year. It had already been three. I hated leaving him at this rough time, but come Monday, I just didn't want to be in the pit.

"Why?" Billy asked.

I told him my lines went off my stock market chart (which shows exact movement) and there was nowhere else to go. In addition, the market had been in a panic all week, I could feel it. "The stock market is going to open down 100 to 125 points today, then we're off the charts into Never Never Land," I informed him.

Billy tried to reassure me, insisting that we sit down and watch the market open together. We called the desk and scheduled a back-up broker for today and Monday. The desk said the call was sixty lower. Later, the market's opening range was from one hundred to one hundred twenty-five points lower. I was right. "See Billy," I said, "I don't want to be there anymore." Truth was, my life was flashing in front of my eyes and I had that bad feeling in the pit of my stomach.

"The MMI has been very good to us," I told him. "I don't want to give it back because of other people's errors." I'd had two errors myself, this week, one bad, one good, and neither were my fault."

Billy stared at me. "If you were to guess, what do you think will happen on Monday?"

I looked him dead in the eyes. "I think the market will open five hundred points lower with total panic. God knows the risk factor is just too big to do this anymore."

On Monday, October 19, 1987, at 8:20 A.M., Billy called me from the exchange floor. The call was five hundred lower, he said, and I shouldn't come in.

"Okay," I laughed, almost hysterically. Pulling the covers over my head, I stayed in bed, shaking. I didn't have to turn on the television. I knew what was happening - a free fall of hysterical proportions and repercussions. No one would fill an order or buy or sell the market. It was all erratic trading and chaotic prices with one side of the pit trading at one price and the other trading at a different price - pure mayhem. In this kind of madness, skill didn't matter. It took pure luck to survive. I was happy to be in bed. No position. No risk.

Just BLACK MONDAY.

Later, I talked to my CME buddies and heard there were guys I knew sitting on the steps of the S&P 500 pit just crying with their hands to their heads. They'd lost it all and then some. My heart broke for them and I had the shakes all day thinking and worrying about my friends. I knew Billy had probably listened to me and got short Friday. He'd covered his position Monday morning and made another slight fortune. Even on Black Monday, everything the man touched turned green. I didn't make any money, but I didn't lose any either. Bottom line, I was alive and happy not to be there, a choice that meant I was still Joyce, Queen of the Mountain.

Chapter Nineteen

THE MUNICIPAL BOND PIT AND THE FBI STING

I took some time off after the crash, in fact, the rest of the year. I had what you call burn-out. The only cure was to walk away from trading for awhile to regain my confidence, intuition, and desire. By January, 1988, I was back on the floor trading Municipal Bonds and the Treasury Bond, mainly from outside the pit. Two of the Bondettes, Midge Townsend and Karen Doherty, were in the Municipal pit filling brokerage. Both were short, petite ladies, one blonde, the other with dark brown hair.

One day I was in the bathroom and Karen comes in. "How's it going?" I ask.

"Not too well," she replies, "my water bag just broke in the pit."

"Oh my God!" I stare at her. "Is there something you want me to do? Should I call the paramedics or your husband?"

"He's on his way to get me," Karen replied, "but could you give these out of range orders to Midge?"

Taking the orders I walked into the pit and delivered them to Midge. "Let me know if you need some help," I told her. A group of orders is called a broker's deck and it works like this. In one pocket, brokers keep the orders close to the market, and in the other, open orders that could be above or below the market. Karen had forgotten to leave all the orders with Midge but somehow remembered before she left for the hospital to give birth. Amazing. I mean I recently read where this pregnant woman thought it was a big deal to be working in a bank, but that's nothing compared to breaking your water bag in the pit at the Chicago Board of Trade with 10,000 men watching. It gives me the chills just to think about it.

The Muni Bond pit where Midge and Karen worked wasn't nearly as busy or volatile as the U.S. Bond pit - likewise your ability to make money there wasn't as great either. Muni and Bonds sat side-by-side because many people spread the Muni against the Bond. It was called the MOB spread. Sometimes, I went there for the economic reports and other times I traded at the clearing house desk of Goldenberg Heymeyer, the company I used to clear my member trades. Their desk sat eight stairs above the Bond pit - a great vantage point to see all the action and my broker. He had dark hair and eyes and at 6'6", towered over everyone at that end of the pit. To help me out, the desk put a tall chair right on the stairwell. I would sit there cross-legged and signal my broker or his assistant. If he bid for something and no one answered, I would sometimes hear him say, "It's for Joy." Nice. And a whole lot easier than standing in that hellhole myself.

In late 1988-89, I had a weird feeling. There were strange vibrations at the exchanges and the rumor mill said there was an investigation underway looking into illegalities in the trading pits. Maybe that explained why I felt like I was being watched when I was in the MMI pit. Later, to my shock, I discovered two things. First, that a man had written a book and used a distorted version of me as his main character. Second, that a girl who'd just started filling brokerage in the bond pit had been virtually destroyed by an FBI sting. She'd adjusted a price on an order to an FBI agent by one tick ($31.25) for a total of $62.50 and they arrested her, using the RICO law to seize her car. Even worse, she was banned from ever trading again. Thank God, it wasn't me, not that I'd ever done anything illegal. Still, maybe I had been lucky to retire on Black Monday.

I felt even luckier as stories started circulating about traders being harassed at home by FBI investigators. I could see that everyone on the floor was getting nervous. Then I started hearing the same thing about the CME floor. Apparently, the FBI was paying late night visits to traders' homes, waking up whole families, questioning them in their pajamas, and scaring their children. They even questioned a guy who was so drunk his wife didn't know how he drove home. The late night interrogations were especially insidious since most traders get up around 5:00 A.M. so they can be on the floor by 6 or 7. I also heard that they threatened one CBOT guy whose wife had just given birth to twins, forcing him to wear a wire while he was trading on the floor. Now, the FBI never did find anything of great value so it all seemed kind of ridiculous.

So ridiculous that it was still on my mind when I went to the movies and saw When Harry Met Sally. The next day while sitting in my favorite coffee shop, I started acting out the film's most famous scene. It's when Sally is pretending to have an orgasm and the woman sitting next to her says, "I'll have what she's having." I'm doing my best to imitate Sally and the whole room is watching me. Then I leaned under the table and in my loudest voice said, "I hope you agents got all that on tape!" The whole coffee shop starts laughing hysterically which put everyone more at ease. Good thing, too. It's hard to work when people are afraid to talk, fearful that anything they say can be used against them. And it would be easy to misinterpret, after all, terminology inside the pit isn't exactly everyday conversation and can be easily misconstrued.

This was validated when a Chicago friend who owned a recording studio was hired by the FBI to check out their secret tapes and testify as to the content. After the trial, he told me about the cross-examination. One of the lawyers asked him questions about a conversation that took place in the pit. My friend laughed and said they really should have asked him about one of the conversations in the background because that's where - in his opinion - something illegal took place.

"Really," I said, "How would you know if you weren't there?"

"The price was wrong," he responded.

Countering, I said the traders might have been checking a trade from ten or twenty minutes before the incident occurred, or they may have been trading a different month in beans. I reminded him that sound travels and you can't tell what part of the pit the speakers are in. Another possibility was that the sound was so loud and distorted on the floor you couldn't distinguish anything. "Would you record music at a football game when the halfback is open and running down the field for a touchdown?" I asked him.

"Gee, Joyce," my friend cringed, "You're probably right. Glad I didn't say the wrong thing."

For these and other reasons, only a handful of clerks and traders were indicted out of our five thousand member traders. Ultimately, the complaints were mostly for false entries on trading cards or for continuing to trade after the final bell rang.

A few people did go to jail on stupid charges which, in my opinion, was unnecessary. One person pleaded guilty to adjusting a tick or two on an order totaling $62.50. Another served six months in jail for making a trade just after the closing bell. Today, it's legal to trade for a couple of minutes after the close. This allows brokers to clear up any missed trades or errors that occurred during the closing bell. It's a good idea because one of the most popular orders in the business is the MOC - market on close - order which is entered into the market just before the close. MOC means buy or sell the quantity at the market on the close only. So an action that used to be wrong is now right. Right? Consider these sentences in light of Goldman Sachs whose last retribution in 2008, was a two million dollar fine and a slap on the wrist. In July, 2010, Goldman was fined five hundred fifty million for hurting every person in the country but did anyone go to jail like the small timers in Chicago? Give me a break - or at least - some justice.

Chapter Twenty

JOHN T. GELDERMANN

Every autumn, the Futures Industry Association (FIA) holds its big convention in Chicago. People from all over the world attend including representatives of the major exchanges, brokerage houses, computer firms, and financial companies. They have booths set up where they display their products and meet with prospective end users. One particular autumn, two of my favorite "Johns" were in attendance. John Damgard, current president of the FIA, was once Vice-President Spiro Agnew's social secretary. He is an old friend of mine from black tie events dating back to the mid-sixties.

The other "John" was John T. Geldermann, Chairman of the Chicago Mercantile Exchange. On this evening, John Gelderman was accompanied by CME director Jeff Silverman, a family friend and one of the brightest men in the commodity business. A graduate of MIT and a large trader in cattle and hogs, Jeff and John G. were co-hosts of a party the CME was holding for the Managed Future Associates (MFA).

John Geldermann was easy to spot in this or any crowd. At 6'3", he had an overpowering appearance with large hands and feet, and broad, well-rounded shoulders. Bald on top with white hair cut short on the sides, John wore wire-rimmed glasses and always dressed in a suit and tie. When he walked into a room everyone noticed him, and if they somehow didn't see him, they couldn't miss his deep voice and soft presentation. Kind of an iron hand in a kid glove. John and his brother, Tom, bought their CBOT memberships back in 1946, and

John purchased a CME membership in 1961.He was chairman of the CME in 1974-75, and again in 1989. He was also chairman of the FIA in 1977-78. The reason John Geldermann held all these positions was that the man really knew his stuff. He also knew exactly what he was doing when, in 1967, he and Tom started a company called CIS, (Computer Information Systems).

CIS pioneered one of the first back-office commodity balancing systems. A balancing system is an electronic system that balances traders' and customers' positions and cash. It also figures the amount of customer and house funds that have to be deposited at the exchanges on a daily basis to cover trading profits, losses, and margin requirements. I used the system when I worked at M-S Commodities and since the program was so new it was no surprise that I found a few bugs. Whenever this happened, I called John and we would help each other out.

John also helped out Leo Melamed when Leo devised the Electronic Globex System for CME. The two were a formidable pair since both men were strong and early proponents of electronic trading. As a result of their efforts, Globex began trading electronically in 1992. Eventually, both the CBOT and NYMEX would list their futures and options products there. John's work also inspired other innovations, including one at CBOT where Billy O'Connor, with the help of Jim Behrens, was developing an electronic trading platform.

Electronic trading was all the buzz and at the party that evening, John and I had a long discussion about how it would impact the pits. Of course, my fellow traders were not too excited about this, not excited at all since CBOT members had taken to wearing badges that showed pit traders with a red line through them and the words "Endangered Species." But as I write this it's 2011, and pit trading is still alive and well. It isn't as busy as electronic trading, but it's persevered as kind of a hybrid and option trade keeps it alive.

Shortly after that party, the CBOT and the CME joined forces to devise a hand held computer for traders inside the pit. The device was called the Automated Data Input Terminal (A.U.D.I.T.). John was co-chairman of the CME Joint Venture A.U.D.I.T.

Committee and Dale Lorenzen was his CBOT counterpart. Since the FBI sting operation in 1988-89, claimed to uncover false entries on member trading cards, both men hoped these little computers would help eliminate fraud. That's why Mr. Geldermann wanted to get traders interested in the project without causing panic and dissension. He cared greatly for the members of both exchanges and for their professional survival. He also decided they would respond better to a woman, a woman they knew and trusted, a woman who was a seasoned trader - ME!

About a year later I met with John. He talked with me about joining the CME where I would help improve the hand held computer since I had a unique talent for catching bugs in computer applications. Intended to replace our existing trading card format, the A.U.D.I.T. was for use inside the trading pit and was designed for trade input only. Seeing, the possibilities, excited to be part of the next wave, I dived right in.

Speaking of waves, John was a big sailor. He had a large, 42 foot sailboat moored at Belmont harbor on beautiful Lake Michigan. He would often invite me to go sailing with him and his sons after the market closed. It was a relaxing to be out on the lake after the daily turmoil. The serene, clear waters and the sun's rays warming our bodies was a therapeutic respite and sometimes an adventure on many summer afternoons.

On one of those afternoons, late July 2006, to be exact, John called at the last minute and asked me to go sailing. Sure, I said. We left the CME at 1:30 PM and made the short drive to Belmont harbor. What was unusual was that it was just the two of us. We motored out of the harbor into the lake and John set the sails. It was there on that gorgeous, peaceful water with our sails in full bloom and the waves breaking off the bow that John told me he only had three months to live. He had completed several different types of chemotherapies. The doctors had told him that the treatments weren't working and they had exhausted every possibility.

Now I understood why we were out here alone. His sons had probably already been informed. The news left me in a rare state of stunned silence. John had been a dear friend and mentor for so many years and I'm happy to say he lived an active life for another five months, five precious months in which his family and friends, including me, could enjoy his company.

On New Year's weekend I called to wish the Geldermann's a happy holiday and found out John wasn't feeling well. I said I wanted to come and see him, but John said no. Then in the background I heard Mrs. Geldermann say "tell Joyce to stop by." With a sinking heart, I immediately dressed and drove to Winnetka, a Chicago suburb, to say goodbye to my dear friend, John. Two days later, he died peacefully surrounded by his large, extended family.

Things were never the same at the Merc, but what John set in motion changed my life - and our business forever. That's the mark of a great man, mentor and friend, and that's why there is still much more to tell about Mr. Geldermann as you'll see when you turn the page.

Chapter Twenty-One

ELECTRONIC TRADING ARRIVES

In 1993, I joined the Chicago Mercantile Exchange staff as part of the Education Department under Deborah Lenchard, Vice President, CME. My first assignment was to test the hand held computer system. Later, I would be tracking traders and teaching members how to use AUDIT in the trading pits. Deb used my expertise in trading and especially, the integration of computers into active floor trading when teaching classes and advanced seminars. Of course, my main focus was to support the Education Department regarding the physical aspects of pit trading including hand signals, carding of trades, market charting, and mock trading sessions. My classes had names like Order Entry and the Interpretation of Orders. These things are the nuts and bolts of trading, things you don't learn in books and must be guided through by an insider. And my insider knowledge always came in handy and gave me good judgement.

When new software came to its beta or testing use phase, I would immediately head for the floor and check it in the pits. Whenever I did this, the MIS (Management Information Department) would take bets on how long it would take me to crash the computer. My average was ten to twelve minutes to hit a bug and crash. Now there were cellular hook-ups all over the floor that took trades directly to the clearing house where those trades were matched. The hand held devices had a hard time keeping up with my trading speed - no surprise - and I worried about how they would maintain the pace of large speculator or floor broker. So I decided my next job was to track a few of the largest.

Through the clearing house, I located the biggest trader on the floor – a Euro Dollar spread local named Norman Byster. And the second biggest? My old friend Don Sliter, he of the MMI pit, once maligned by the Bondettes. Since I knew both men, it made it easy for me to sweet talk them into letting me shadow them and enter their trades.

Norman Byster was a very good looking man about 6'6" with dark hair and eyes. A big, husky 230 pounds, Norman was more like a football player than a mathematical genius. (I'd dated Norman years before, right after I broke my engagement to Doug.) As I think about him, I realize that a lot of important men in this business are actually soft-spoken people. Sure, they can yell, but that isn't their normal, everyday style. Norman was really sort of quiet and even a little bashful. It was very appealing along with his huge mind, a mind he applied brilliantly.

As a spread trader in the Euro Dollar contract, Norman bought and sold spreads and sometimes legged them or had a broker fill one end of the spread for him. Basically, he traded the interest rate yield curve. For example, he would buy September Euro Dollars, then go to the December contract and sell them. If he could leg the spread for a tick better than the spread market bid and offer quoted, he could make a tick. Norman traded 1,000 lot contracts at a time. If he could leg the spread by a tick better (a tick was worth $25.00), the 1000 contracts entry would equal a $25,000 gain. In addition, Norman could immediately sell the spread as a spread and keep the profit or, he could potentially make more money later on the yield curve change. He could also leg the spread off and maybe make another tick for $50,000. Norman was living proof that there are many ways to profit from a transaction besides whether the market goes up and down.

I had used my powers of persuasion to convince Norman to let me stand behind him in the busy Euro pit. From this prime location, I would use the handheld's writing recognition to enter his trades as if they were mine. This allowed me to test the speed and accuracy of the computer versus writing onto a trading card, but I had a problem right away. The hand held device only had enough room in the "Quantity" space to enter 999 contracts. Uh-oh! Norman traded thousand lots! That meant every single time he made a trade, I had to enter two trades, one for 999 and one with identical information for a single lot. Norman would look over his shoulder, see me writing quickly, copiously, and wonder what the hell was taking me so long - especially with everybody watching. He was peeved because this was the bad part of live trade tracking. By watching me, the other traders knew every time Norman made a trade - but that's what this testing was all about, I thought, - working out the kinks and clumsiness of electronic trading. So I continued to do my job, closely mimicking Norman's trading pattern and habits, even his comings and goings from the pit.

It wasn't easy on either of us, all the more reason I was happy Norman had patience and a gentleman's disposition. Unfortunately, some of the pit members didn't share these attributes. They kept complaining and asking Norman why he was letting me track his trades. Whenever this happened, he would turn around and say, "Ask Joyce." Then I would answer them truthfully, saying "I sweet talked Norman into letting me follow his cute ass around." Norman would just smile as he left the pit with me following close behind. After all, I was trying to be an accurate tester and exactly duplicate the rigors of the trading day. Suddenly Norman stopped. "Test it anywhere," his eyes twinkled as he turned to me and the guys, " Except here." Then he walked into the men's room. Resolute, I stood by the door and waited for him to come out.

One day while working with Norman in Euro Dollars, a husky, 6'6" trader brought a whipped cream pie into the pit and mashed it in his best friend's face. The friend, himself 6'3" with whipped cream plastered all over his head, shoulders, and beautiful red hair, jumps on the perpetrator, gets him in a leg lock, and retaliates in kind. We were laughing hysterically, but it was a mess and not exactly floor protocol so they both got in trouble. The CME had just installed trial security surveillance cameras in the Euro Dollar area for out-trade purposes and those cameras had caught the pie action. We all headed to the security office to see re-runs of the pit incident and again we all laughed hysterically. Trading is so high stress that it's good to have some humor now and then. Fortunately, both traders involved were nice guys and buddies who'd stood next to each other for years so no harm done.

Maybe.

The next morning I was standing in the pit when Mr. Pie Thrower made the market (the first open out-cry bid) and a broker didn't trade with him. I told Mr. Pie, "If that broker had overlooked me, he would be eating his teeth and if I was your size, who knows what I would have done."

Pie thrower and his friend standing next to him both laughed and said," Yeah, that's what we heard about you JOY."

"Nobody, but nobody is going to rain on my parade or miss me when I make a market," I declared.

I discussed my observations, insights, and progress during my numerous weekly AUDIT meetings with Mr. Geldermann - and I didn't only meet with him. I regularly met with the CME computer department and the Executive Committee. We also met monthly with the CME member committee and the Joint Venture Member Committee at the CBOT. It seems a few CBOT traders were making minimal use of the hand held device but not doing it consistently or pushing it to the max like me. This meant I was the only one getting a handle on the unit's flaws and problems and I took this knowledge into my next trial with Don Sliter.

By now, Sliter was the second largest trader at the CME. He was a large scalper which means he got in and out of trades quickly. Don had traded with me in the MMI and I would always kid and tease him good-naturedly. And it was good-natured because I consider Sliter one of my best friends in the business. Don used to trade in the S&P pit from the opening at 8:30 AM until 9:30 AM, then come back and trade from 1:30 PM until the close at 3:15. He only traded two and a half to three hours a day, but did more trades in this short time then most people did all day. In fact one day, I clocked Sliter at seventeen trades a second. He was so lightening quick that it was impossible for me to follow him accurately and completely track his trades. Sliter's trade check clerk actually had other clerks lined up to check their broker's trades with Sliter the whole time he was in the pit trading. At one point, I lost track and had to ask him to tell me when he was flat, that is, when he had no position in the market. Ten minutes go by and he is still trading like crazy. "Hey!" I remind him, "you were supposed to tell me when you were flat."

Sliter turned, smiled, and said, "JOY, I'm never flat."

The handheld's hardware had been designed by Seiko of Japan. Two members of their design team visited the CME to see how the device was working. I took them down on the floor to do a live demonstration. I wanted them to see some of the strange things that occur during trading hours. The pair was totally impressed with the trading and the wild people running everywhere. They loved the screaming and hand waving even though they didn't have a clue what it meant.

Sliter walked over and I introduced him to the two Japanese designers. "Kochira wa Sliter-San desu. S&P pit no nako ni Sliter-San ichi ban takai trader desu." Awestruck, the two gentlemen immediately gave a huge bow.

Sliter raised his eyebrows. "What did you say?"

"I told them you are the number one biggest, highest point trader inside the S&P pit."

"That's true," Sliter nodded in agreement.

"Ahhh." To our surprise, the two men bowed twice.

Of course, they understood English and they were so impressed with Sliter that meeting him made their day. I knew this because I had studied Japanese and the Japanese people for several years. They go out of their way to be polite and show how impressed they are with important individuals like they did with Sliter-San of the S&P.

At the time, dozens of Globex trading computers were set up on stairs at the north end of the S&P pit. In fact, the first main Globex contract was the MINI S&P. The guys trading on Globex would watch the pit and attempt to pick off the traders. In other words, if they saw a large order, they would try to beat the trader to Globex. The pit traders got very aggravated at this so eventually, all the electronic terminals placed around the pits were moved.

My nephew, Wally, had recently come to the CME from the CBOT Bond pit to trade the NASDAQ. I said, "Go into the S&P pit at the opening and watch Sliter."

"What's a Sliter?" Wally asked sarcastically.

"You'll figure it out," I answered.

The next morning I ran into my nephew and asked if he'd found Sliter.

Wally looks at me like I'm stupid and says, "Of course, in the first ten minutes, he traded with every guy in the pit."

Exactly what I wanted my nephew to see - how Sliter differed from the other three hundred traders in the S&P pit. Later that day I saw the man himself.

"Your nephew was in the pit watching me today," Sliter said.

I couldn't believe he'd had time to notice Wally, but I wasn't surprised. Sliter is amazing and my nephew trades just like him. I mean, how do they move so fast? Maybe Wally's 6'5", long armed body, blonde hair and deep voice help him get noticed. My accountant was talking about Wally one day and said he's never seen a youngster in this business make so much money so fast.

The Euro Dollar and S&P pits were always extremely crowded and quite noisy, and this was the best time to pay a visit with the handheld. In business clothes with my trading jacket or in the purple jacket of the education department, I would descend into the chaos. The pushing and shoving, the ringing of the land line and cell phones all affected the AUDIT's performance. Sometimes, my electronic pen would shoot electrical lines across the input screen messing up a trade I was trying to enter, other times the screen would go completely blank.

My computer expert in Management Information Systems, (MIS, now called IT, Information Technology) was Mike Boggess. Mike made changes on the software and corrected any bugs I found. In one of our weekly meetings, he said he'd like to go down on the floor with me. He wanted to test the device himself by making some trades and seeing first hand what interference took place on the trading screen. I thought it was a good idea. With two of us on the job, finding the errors would be easier so we could get Seiko to correct the problems.

John Geldermann and the head of MIS gave their approval so Mike and I made plans to go down and do some testing in the Swiss Franc pit.

I'd found a big trader there who agreed to let me stand behind him and enter his trades. The Swiss franc pit is smaller with just a few steps down but that was perfect for Mike's maiden voyage. Excited, the two of us headed in to do the test in this currency environment. We wore our CME jackets and appeared to belong in the trading area. Before we went in, I gave Mike strict instructions – Don't stand directly behind anyone. Don't talk unless they ask you a question. If I say out, immediately step off the trading pit."

"Got it," Mike took a deep breath, "I'm ready."

Walking into the pit, I stood right behind the local trader who'd agreed to let me observe him. He was tall and slender, a quiet young guy and the biggest trader in the Swiss Franc pit. Mike stood near a short, stocky floor broker.

"Are you watching me?" the broker challenged Mike

"No," Mike said, "I am entering synthetic trades into a computer for testing purposes."

Twenty minutes later, the same broker yells at another trader and I scream for Mike to get OUT!

Quickly, Mike exits and just in time – a fistfight is breaking out right where he was standing between the stocky broker and a guy who ran across the pit from the other side. The combatants are rolling down the stairs throwing punches. It was truly funny and I was trying not to laugh too hard at all the yelling, screaming, and predictable bad language. I had the distinct impression that these two traders had had "issues" before. While they duked it out, I continued to stand behind my trader and we watched everyone else break up the fight.

Later, Mike asked me, "Why didn't you move?"

"Because," I said, "I was behind the tallest, largest trader in the pit and believe me, no one was going to touch him or piss him off. You, on the other hand, picked a short, feisty guy who is probably always getting into fights." Of course, I was right and that is what experience will do for you. These types of incidents - loud screaming, cussing, fists flying - happen all the time. You just have to know where to stand and who will protect you.

It was especially appropriate for Mike to learn this lesson. My computer geek is 5'4" tall and weighs about 140 pounds. He has dark brown hair and eyes to match, eyes that are always smiling and sparkling, even from behind his wire rimmed glasses. Mike also has the advantage of being slim and fast on his feet, I mean, he got out of that pit in split second time. I know the experience taught him a lot about trading, the handheld, life, and later that night, made for great conversation with his charming wife, Linda. I would've loved to have heard Mike's version of the story and someday I will as we frequently talk over lunch. In addition, Mike's family often stays at my place during the world class Chicago Marathon. His son runs the race and we all watch and cheer the young man on. Mike and I are at the CBOT now, and we still laugh about our adventure in the Swiss franc pit that day and talk about our colleagues, like Sliter.

These days, Sliter is primarily an electronic trader, but he occasionally enters the S&P pit and comes in for certain government reports. When I talked to Norman Byster about a year ago, he too, was trading electronically from home and had cut way back on the size of his position. What does it say that so many open out cry experts have gone electronic?

In my opinion, the pit with open out cry has many attributes electronic trading doesn't. When the Chicago Board of Trade started its electronic trading system (similar to Globex), I told Billy O'Connor, CBOT Chairman at the time, "Electronics make it too easy to cheat - no one's watching you." By contrast, in the pit everyone watches everyone. The banks watch the brokerage houses. The brokerage houses watch the trading desks. The trading desks tell customers what's going on and everybody knows everybody else's business. With electronic trading, I don't know what's going on until it's too late.

Occasionally, John Geldermann and I would go down to the floor to make some electronic trades. It was hard for him to use the handheld. John has very large hands so he could hold the thing but inputting the trade was difficult. He'd been shot in the forearm during World War

II and it was almost impossible for him to position the pen to write on the screen. John would input just a few hog or cattle trades then his hand would start cramping. He'd give up, smile charmingly and thank God he was too old to go into the pit anymore, with or without a computer.

It makes me wonder, will electronic traders someday say the same thing?

Chapter Twenty-Two

TAKE YOUR DAUGHTERS TO WORK DAY

Around 1996, businesses across the country began hosting "Take Your Daughters to Work Day." At the Chicago Mercantile Exchange this became a big event because the young ladies were fascinated by the flash and frenzy of the trading pits - just like me! Every year we had a great turnout with over three hundred girls participating in our special program. Why so many? Besides the members, the Merc employed thousands of IT personnel, trading clerks, price recorders, security, and many other professionals. Since I was on the Education Committee, I oversaw the pit trading aspect of the day and was eager to pass my knowledge onto a new generation of potential female traders.

On one particular Take Your Daughters to Work Day, I was waiting for the girls to arrive when someone called in an anonymous bomb threat. The exchange received these calls with sad regularity. We members had learned to take them in stride and to trust the Merc security department to manage the situation. Most of the time, the CME didn't even make an official announcement of the threat but word would get out and it would become casual conversation on the floor. For the most part, these incidents were more a nuisance than a threat. It only became a member concern when security declared the need to clear the trading floor and this was rare. In fact, I only remember once in forty years when a threat brought trading to a halt. It was at the CBOT and only lasted one hour.

But today we couldn't take any chances. Many of the girls had arrived with their fathers before 6 A.M. We were already nervous about handling so many children and the bomb threat only intensified the situation. More girls kept showing up and we knew even more would arrive by the end of the day. The turnout was bigger than we expected.

Suddenly, at 8:30 AM, a second bomb threat came in just as the S&P 500 futures market was about to open. Members were notified but trading started on time. As usual, the traders focused on their work and didn't pay much attention to the threat. But for safety reasons and to be responsive to parents' concerns, the CME decided to remove the girls from the exchange building and take them to - WHERE? WHERE CAN YOU DROP IN WITH 300 GIRLS?

Fortunately, Jack Sandner, Chairman of the CME, had a brilliant Plan B. He called the Lyric Opera of Chicago which is located directly across the street. For years, the relationship between our two institutions had flourished. Jack spoke to Ardis Krainik's office, describing the situation - 300 girls with nowhere to go - asking for any help and guidance she could offer. Ardis was a former mezzo-soprano opera singer who was presently general director of the Lyric and like any good general from Eisenhower to Colin Powell, she marshaled her resources and sprang into action.

Immediately, Ardis said they'd make room for us. She told Jack to bring the girls over to their rehearsal hall right away. Since we already had police and bomb sniffing dogs on the scene at the CME, the police helped us move the girls - small group by small group - safely out of the exchange and across the street to their new meeting place at Lyric Opera.

The wonder of the experience was immediate as the girls were transported on a huge industrial elevator used to move big scenery, props, and instruments up to the rehearsal level. It took about thirty minutes of quick maneuvering to move them all, but we arrived safely without incident or lost children. The Lyric rehearsal hall was a large room with few chairs and no real seating to speak of. This was because the hall was actually a stage setup area with high ceilings to project and enhance sound. Fascinating, but not part of our planned day for the girls. Did I say plans? What plans? Our arrangements had been blown to smithereens and now we had to think on our feet. It was total pandemonium with hundreds of teenaged girls and their high pitched voices amplified throughout the space. (Ooops! Was this what I sounded like when my voice projected into the corn pit?)

But to our delight and pleasure there were some singers from the Lyric Opera's Center of American Artists in the hall rehearsing. One of them was David Cangelosi, a noted tenor who specialized in comprimario singing. He is well known for playing funny and entertaining parts, having starred as Mime in Wagner's Siegfried and as Toby in Sweeney Todd. I've heard David perform both parts and he was wonderful. He sang to the girls for at least an hour and they have no idea how lucky they were to see him engaging with them, so up close and personal. I could see that he enjoyed entertaining them, too.

Entertaining, not to mention holding the attention, of three hundred mostly high school and a few younger aged (7 - 11) girls for an hour is an amazing feat. It was incredible how they all sat quietly, cross legged on the floor, laughing and enjoying his acapella performance of clowns and funny people from the opera as more girls kept arriving. Finally, David finished.

Now it was our turn to perform. The main event of the day was the mock trading session hosted by the Education Department and Vice President, Deborah Lenchard. After all, trading or assisting the traders is what these girls' moms and dads did for a living, so we wanted to expose them to the profession. We broke the girls into age groups and several exchange members, mainly females, taught them hand signals face to face. They acted out how to buy and sell, using their hands to signal positions and quantities. The members then showed them how to card (write down) a trade. After this individual instruction period, the girls were ready to go.

We placed them in a large circle on the floor. The tallest girls were in the outside row with the smaller girls toward the middle. The real young ones stood in the center. Quickly, we re-rehearsed the buy, sell, quantities, and hand signals. Now, we were ready to do some live trading. It was fantastic, not to mention invigorating with everyone screaming at the top of their lungs. The sound was so high pitched that I felt right at home and while the girls were deafening, I must confess I could out scream them all. I loved it! Especially since I was also busy directing and pointing out girls who were trying to get other girls' attention so they could trade with them.

As I walked around helping the girls card their trades correctly, the opera singers stayed to watch, surprised at how loud and fast the girls could be. The singers were especially amazed by the girls' sound projection, their hands waving, and voices screaming numbers and prices. How did these youngsters figure out what was going on, who was buying, who was selling and do it so quickly? The girls rapidly caught onto the need for concentration and focus. Trading proved so intriguing and exciting that even the littlest ones wanted to take a chance and speculate. While I'm sure the tiniest didn't have a clue what "speculate" means, they knew what FUN meant and that's all that counted.

I could see how excited they were and knew they couldn't wait to tell their parents how much money they'd made. Some made $10, others $100, and one girl claimed she made a million dollars. I tried to hire her to work for me but her dad said no way. In any case, we all had a great time and the day went pretty smoothly considering the bomb scare, the fear, confusion and the location change. The next year the mock trading session was an equally unbelievable, unforgettable experience since the girls were able to use the huge EuroDollar pit which I describe as being shaped like the ship of fools.

Except that the daughters weren't foolish at all. They were all smart cookies, as were their brothers, which is why the CME created a similar day for members' sons.

For me, it was a great experience, and I wondered as I said goodbye, was one of these girls the next Queen of the Mountain? I hoped so, and I hoped she would love this business as much as I did.

Chapter Twenty-Three

FOREIGN CUSTOMERS AND MOCK TRADING

My department - the Chicago Mercantile Exchange Education Department - was responsible for hosting various educational seminars and mock trading sessions for professional groups. During the 1994 World Cup Soccer Championship, hosted by the United States, delegates from the competing countries poured into Chicago including visitors from Brazil, England, Niger, Argentina, Spain, and other nations. The CME held a cocktail party on the exchange floor and about fifteen hundred of these people attended. We'd arranged for a very special event midway though the party - a mock trading session in which all attendees could participate.

Reluctantly, a few guests stepped forward. Very few. Then, what really helped was that some of our members attending the party came forward. Seeing our members join in gave more guests confidence. Suddenly, the rush was on as about five hundred people wanted to participate. As always with these sessions, fun and hilarity ruled. Little cultural groups formed in the pit, but what made this session different from so many others was that the numbers were shouted in the languages of the world - Portuguese, Japanese, Spanish, English, and many more. It was a Babel of voices and so uplifting to see these diverse people speaking diverse languages while doing the same thing. They were all learning, laughing, and enjoying themselves.

We held a similar cocktail party and mock trading session for several hundred members of the California delegation, in town for the

Democratic National Convention in the summer of 1996. The CME
had become a must see for any professional group visiting Chicago
and we did our best to show off commodity trading as a necessary and
exciting part of business and life in the Windy City. Many of us carried
that message around the world.

I was visiting Costa Rica with a group from Chicago's famous
Lincoln Park Zoo. We went there to study and observe the life cycles
of various avian species. Otherwise known as Birding. Yes, Birding.
On this trip, we were studying various species of extinct, rare, and
common birds, bats, and ants in the rain forest. (The ants and their life
cycle were a surprising and interesting addition to the trip, especially
how they marched and the regimentation of their colony, which is very
similar to our bees and their queen.)

It was one of my favorite trips, especially when we visited a small
farm community and spent the day at a local school. It was a very small
grammar school with only eighty children. The school building was
an old, one story wood frame structure with four or five classrooms
and one lunchroom. Surrounding the school was a dirt playground and
across the road, what looked like farmland growing corn. The students
had entertained us and now it was our turn to entertain them. What
should we do?

One man suggested ring-around-the-rosey. I said, "I have something
I could do that the kids would really enjoy. Let's do a mock trading
session." Another man rolled his eyes as if to say "oh please!" But I
was confident the kids would enjoy it. I knew they had seen television
or live village auctions before with open out-cry on cars, cattle, and
grains. (Just think about Amsterdam where they have flower auctions in
the marketplace.) Bidding and offering to finally arrive at a fair market
price is a universal language. Since there was a cornfield next to the
school, I decided to mock trade corn. They gave me an interpreter to
help explain what we were doing so all the children could understand
and participate.

Most of the kids did not speak English, but I could count to one
hundred in Spanish and speak a little of the language as well. This
meant we had enough in common to get started. The children knew

they were going to buy and sell a commodity, corn, and the interpreter explained a few things I was saying. I divided the students into a buy group and a sell group. In ten minutes, I had them trading corn at two dollars and fifty cents a bushel, then 51-52 cents, and finally selling at 53-54. They were all screaming, yelling, jumping up and down and quoting the prices in Spanish. Even the teachers got into it and followed my every move. It was so much fun, the highlight of the trip. My fellow tour members were amazed at how well it turned out and how much the children enjoyed trading. Not that much of a surprise really - what child (and admit it, what adult) wouldn't enjoy screaming, yelling, and jumping up and down? Especially at school.

The kids got so excited that their enthusiasm even carried over to ring-around-the-rosey, although I suspect they enjoyed trading more. You see, the act of trading seems to come naturally. It's an ability that spans all cultures and is for people of all ages. Even if they don't comprehend what's really going on, people know something significant is happening so they enter into the act with gusto.

And that's what trading - and life - really require.

Chapter Twenty-Four

AGRICULTURAL CUSTOMERS

In 1998, the CME decided to downsize by laying off two hundred people. One by one, the Education Department was dissolved and handheld training was moved to another department. I was replaced by three -three!- youngsters with no trading experience. I knew this wouldn't work for the same reason John Geldermann knew it wouldn't work. To push a new trading procedure like the handheld through, the members needed a person they could relate to. Soon the project ended and I was hired by Jack Sandner's firm, RB&H Financial, to handle agricultural customers on the CME floor.

John F. Sandner, known to his friends as Jack, is a nine-term Chairman of the Chicago Mercantile Exchange. A short, smiling, blue-eyed Irishman, his best quality is that he's a vibrant, uplifting man who's great to be around. Jack and his wife adopted seven children and their spirit of generosity, of wanting to help kids get on the right track, came from Jack's early life experience as a high school drop-out. On this path to nowhere, Jack met Tony Zale, the Middleweight Champion of the world. Tony befriended Jack and the relationship changed Jack's life. Not only did Tony teach him to be a disciplined amateur boxer with a record of 58-2, Jack became a Golden Gloves champion. He won an athletic scholarship to the University of Arizona and attended Notre Dame Law School. Upon graduation, Jack started practicing and trading pork bellies, but the lure of trading proved irresistible and commodities became his life just like it had become mine.

Jack was interviewed about his trading success in the book "the Inner Game of Trading" by Robert Koppel and Howard Abell. He says, and I quote, "If you have this tremendous fear of failing (you've got to have a reasonable amount of fear to do well), if the fear is overwhelming, you won't do well. You will do things that are unnatural and then you will fail. So you have to have balance. It's just like going into the boxing ring and you're so afraid of losing or getting knocked out that you run all the time. You're going to lose! But if you have enough fear to make you perform well then that fear is good fear, but you can't allow yourself to be controlled by the fear."

They also asked Jack what separates the traders from people who are able to make it time and time again to the finish line. Jack summarized his thoughts with this, "The fear of losing and greed. Focus gives you discipline and self-confidence, and ultimately, success."

As colleagues, those were qualities Jack and I shared. Our customers shared them too, especially our agricultural customers who were a breed unto themselves (no pun intended). Here's what I mean.

In my previous chapters I've described the different types of people who trade commodities. Topping the list of good, fun, knowledgeable traders/hedgers are my Iowa farm boys and they're not what you think. In fact, farmers aren't anything like they're depicted on television or in the movies. Yes, most of them are down-to-earth, All-American college boys but they also have a keen business sense and know how to hedge their crop financially. A hedge is a position established in the futures market to offset market exposure and price fluctuations. It minimizes your exposure to unwanted price risk. If a farmer sells a number of soybean future contracts equal to his crop size at planting, he effectively locks in the price of his soybeans at that time. For example, if the man feels his soybeans are worth eight dollars a bushel, he can use the futures market to secure that price.

For the most part, Iowa farmers are looking to lock in the two products they grow corn or soybeans, but they also have livestock including hogs, cattle, cows, and chickens. My one customer had a lot of milking cows and often traded milk futures along with his cattle, corn, and soybeans. I was talking to him one morning before the market opened and he sounded like he was catching a cold. I asked if he had the sniffles. To my shock, he started crying.

"No," his voice filled with genuine emotion, "My favorite cow died this morning. I walked in and found her lying on the barn floor, dead. She was the best cow I ever had. She always gave me more milk than all the other cows, and she would smile into my eyes, happy to see me each morning. Lately," He went on," I've been worried about her. She seemed to be moving a little slower and hasn't quite been up to par. I had Doc, the veterinarian, here yesterday. He checked her out and said the only problem was that she was getting old."

I was amazed to see such deep emotions pouring out of him over a cow's death. He may have been an aggressive trader/hedger, but he cared a great deal about life and animals. His cows gave him milk and in return he took excellent care of them. The man had tremendous pride in his livestock and his work. I was impressed with his sense of honor and the courage it took to share his feelings.

By contrast, Farmer Mike was younger and always cracking jokes. He'd planted a large acreage of grains on his land and raised a lot of swine. Mike would tell me funny, smelly pig stories while we were trading grains. He had an aggressive style and when he wasn't planting or working in the fields, he liked to speculate. Mike and a few buddies had set up a small trading office in some small Iowa town where they used to hang out and trade.

One week while I was on vacation, Mike managed to lose fifty thousand dollars. Being his normal, aggressive self without me there to say "Whoa!" and reign him in had gotten Mike in trouble.

"Don't worry, Joyce," he grinned when I asked him about it, "I 'll get it back. I sent you twenty thousand dollars yesterday and I'll borrow the rest against my crop."

Except that Mike was long in the wheat contract and the wheat market didn't look too good. In fact, it looked pretty weak. I was nervous for him. I mean Mike was my customer, my responsibility and I would have to pay for his loss if something went wrong. A few days later, the market opened and like a bat out of hell, wheat went straight Limit UP - as high as a contract can trade in one day. Mike starts screaming, yelling, celebrating and had his whole little office laughing and trading. He then sells twice the amount of wheat he had bought and was now short wheat at limit up. The market broke ten cents and immediately, Mike bought his short position back. He did the same trade twice that day and made about thirty thousand dollars. Mike was on a roll and very quickly made up all his losses.

Shortly after his big trading day, Mike and a few farm buddies came to Chicago to celebrate. They visited the CME floor and I introduced them to several of the big traders they'd heard so much about. Later, we went out for cocktails on Rush Street where we ran into even more traders. Lubricated by liquor, the conversation and the jokes flowed so fast and furious that my sides still hurt from laughing so hard.

As we walked into our second bar of the night there, at the first table, were three pretty, young, girls who had just sat down. Seeing them, Mike walked over and offered to buy them a drink.

"Hi," he said, "I'm Mike from Iowa. May I buy you ladies a drink?"

They looked at him like he was some kind of hick (wrong) then one of them said, "Sure, why not." After all, there were three of them but only one Mike.

Mike paid for their drinks, said "Goodbye, nice meeting you" and returned to our table. He didn't speak to them again. Turns out, he just wanted to be kind to some pretty ladies. His buddy said Mike does this all the time. I smiled, thinking again that my Iowa farmers are THE BEST, just good old all-American boys who want to have fun. I also think that working around crops and natural cycles gave them great insights into timing.

I've said it before and I'll say it again, in trading, timing is everything. Whether you're trading commodities, stocks, or cars, to be successful, you have to watch the timing of economic indicators and the way they change from year to year. I mean, one day these factors have great importance, and the next week, not so much. That's why you have to watch the reports for the revisions on the previous month's figures. You must also be aware of what various analysts and traders are expecting to find in the numbers. Remember, movements in other commodities can directly effect your position. While I was trading U.S. Bonds, I constantly watched the price fluctuations and movement of crude oil throughout the day.

Crude oil has an enormous impact on interest rates and inflation worldwide. I've been observing the crude oil markets for so many years that I've gained great insight and a feeling for the adjacent natural gas commodity market, too. Often, there are similarities between trading oil and trading natural gas, but each is capable of making fast and unpredictable moves on its own.

My partner had a large cattle customer, Tom, who had oil and natural gas on his land. Many cattle ranchers in Texas have oil wells spread across their property. When you drill these wells looking for oil, you hit natural gas first. You then have to tap the gas before the oil drilling process can continue. Tom had been hedging or speculating in the natural gas market and was a net loser at about $218,000. I knew this because my partner was on vacation and I was keeping an eye on his customers, Tom included. For this I needed - and had - eyes in the back of my head. You see, many cattlemen and feed lot operators trade in all three markets - oil, natural gas, and a crop or livestock. Tom, the cattle trader, fit in this category. He was very short positioned in the gas market and the price was not going down as he predicted, in fact, it kept moving higher.

One morning I was watching the crude oil market when I noticed that natural gas was looking very weak. I had a feeling it was going to break and the NYMEX was about to back me up. You see, the CME floor has live commodity quote boards coming from the New York Mercantile Exchange (NYMEX) where oil and gas are traded. When I concentrate one hundred percent on these boards, it's like I'm there on the New York floor and my instincts get really good. I wanted to get Tom out of his bad, losing position so I put all my focus on his position liquidation and not on my own personal gains. I probably should have sold some natural gas for my own trading account, but it would have been a conflict of interest to position myself when I was about to do a large liquidation for a customer. Besides, I wanted to keep a clear head, use my common sense and market knowledge unclouded by the anticipation of making or losing money for myself.

I called Tom, revved on adrenaline. "Tom," I said, "are your ready to ROCK AND ROLL?"

"What do you mean, Joyce?" he asked cautiously.

"Traders and speculators are about to kick the hell out of the natural gas market," I said, "so get your liquidation orders ready. We are momentarily going to dump your damn losing trade. My palms are itching and that means we're about to make a lot of money."

"But Joyce," Tom protested, "even though my system is delayed seven minutes, my quote screen shows that nothing is happening."

"It will," I assured him. Then I told Tom to get the orders ready and I would call him back in a few minutes.

Suddenly, it starts and BANG! There it is, Tom's big chance to get out of that two hundred thousand dollar loss. I was right. The bottom is falling out. People are pulling their buy orders and natural gas is going all sellers. Speed is of the essence. I call the NYMEX floor on my direct line and dial Tom at the same time. I order the phone clerk next to me to watch my phones since I'm going to MOVE SOME SIZE IN NEW YORK! I have a phone in each ear and an order ready to write and time stamp. I give the latest gas quote to Tom and say, "What's your first order?" He gives me a quantity to buy at his first price and I tell him the market is already trading below that price.

Tom says, "Buy ten at the market!" (Buying "at the market" means paying whatever the selling price is).

I put in an order for his account to buy ten November natural gas contracts at the market and at the same time I ask Tom for his next order. He gives it to me and I say, "We're already through that price."

"Buy ten at the market," he shouts in my ear, "no, make it twenty!"

I tell New York, "Buy twenty at the market."

The speed gets faster, more urgent. There's no time for conversation, only to take orders. We're in a free fall market with arms spread wide and Tom's position is improving. He gives me more orders. We are making money. The next two are below market and in a few seconds they are filled too.

Tom tells me his quotes are finally starting to go down and we both laugh because he has already made back the two hundred thousand dollars. On the way down, I constantly quote the last two digits of the price so Tom can see how fast the market is falling. His quotes from me are immediate, live from the clerk in the pit. Except that the market is falling so fast that my quotes are erratic and not totally in correct order 90, 89, 85, 82, 75, 70, and 65. It's hard to keep completely up to speed but it was good enough to get Tom out. Finally, I said, "Tom let's do it. Give me the final order. You will be flat (no position) and make a profit." He did, and in a matter of minutes that final order was filled. Seven minutes to be exact.

That's right, in seven minutes Tom had made two hundred and thirty-seven thousand dollars. We'd made back his debit loss plus about eighteen thousand dollars in profits. No sooner had we completed his last transaction then the market started going up. In no time, it was right back to where it was when I called him. What had occurred was a fast break down and an even faster rally up, otherwise known as a spike. During this particular spike, there was a seven minute window to cover short positions and we got in before that window closed, just in the nick of time.

And by the time Tom's delayed quote board was quoting the market at the bottom, the futures were already back up to where they were when we started getting ready to liquidate. Tom had been very worried about the large loss he'd incurred and last night, had even called me at home to discuss it. Today that conversation had a happy ending. Tom was grateful to recoup and make a small profit too. He didn't need to be greedy.

In the movie "Wall Street", Gordon Gekko, played by Michael Douglas, says "Greed is good." But Tom and I knew that wasn't true. Greed floods you with self-absorption that finally ends in self-destruction. It will always bring you grief, especially when it causes you to lose money because you've stayed in a position too long.

My customers and I prefer the other side - honest trading and terrific gut instinct. In other words, if you have a good feeling, go with it or as they say, if you got a hunch, buy a bunch. That's what I did and it helped me save Tom a lot of money he might have lost. It was that trader feeling, that intuition. I saw the break coming before it began and I sprang into action, happy to help.

It's amazing to me that from start to finish that action took seven minutes, seven minutes to get my customer out of a horrific loss. Now if that loss was the sundae, Tom's eighteen-thousand dollar profit was the whipped cream and cherry on top. Was it any wonder we had a sweet tooth?

Chapter Twenty-Five

9/11

It's Monday, September 11, 2001, about 7:45 AM, Central Standard Time. I'm about to walk out of my condominium and head to work. As I reach for the remote to turn off the TV, a special report comes on - the World Trade Center's north tower has just been hit by a commercial airliner! Oh, my God! Traders should be arriving at those offices NOW preparing to go onto the trading floor! I can hardly breathe as I realize how many of these traders and their member firms I KNOW. A sick feeling starts in the pit of my stomach as I watch the World Trade Center Complex that houses these branch offices BURN! Forcing myself to move, I run out of my condominium, jump in a cab and reach the Chicago Mercantile Exchange in record time.

Immediately, I know something is wrong - very wrong. On a normal day, this exchange is packed with people sprinting for their offices or the trading floor and the din is deafening. Instead, it's so quiet I can hear my own heart beat. Feeling off kilter I try to steady myself as I enter the elevator. There on the wall is a small television screen that flashes news updates and headlines all day long. It's about 8:05AM. Five people are crowded in behind me. Suddenly a news brief flashes across the screen - a second airliner has hit the World Trade Center's south tower!

Gasping, I look around as each person's eyes fill with horror. Our jaws hit the floor but no one makes a sound. We are all thinking the same thing - our friends, our colleagues! Like me, everyone here knows someone there. A lot of someones, - friends, sweethearts, business associates who work at the WTC. Desperately, I thank God that the markets aren't open yet. Maybe some of my people have escaped! I pray that they are out in the streets, trying to get to their offices just like I'm trying to get to mine. But as I exit the elevator, I don't walk into my office, I walk into pandemonium.

The CME is evacuating the entire building and the trading floor NOW even though there are already two thousand traders and clerks on that floor waiting for trading to begin. Immediately, activity on CME's Globex Electronic Trading System halts even though it has been active all night with heavy European trading. Eurdollars and currencies go on delayed opening (and stay that way for three days!) and the CME announces that the trading pits won't open. Across the country, the NYSE, NYBOT, COMEX, NYMEX, and CBOT all close down. On the floor of the CME, phones are ringing off the hook but nobody answers because the exchange has ordered everybody out - Ourbuilding is a high risk target!

Horrified traders and clerks scramble, realizing that the Chicago Mercantile Exchange is a mini-World Trade Center, a lookalike, with our two tower buildings projecting skyward and our exchange resting in between. Were we next? The idea is an invitation to terror, especially with the country and the markets in total chaos. In the midst of all this panic, the CME moves quickly and efficiently to get us out of harm's way.

In Chicago, we all make it out alive. Sadly, this wasn't the case in New York, the Pentagon, or that Pennsylvania field. But there's more to the story. Did you know three buildings - not two - exploded and collapsed at the World Trade Center complex? The third in what almost looks like a controlled demolition? Check any of the websites showing WTC Building #7 going down or Fox News or any of the other news outlets. Anyway you look at it, the collapse of Building #7 is extremely frightening because you can't really see what caused it. There was a fire at that location earlier in the day, but if you look closely, you see a slight explosion on the first floor, then the second, the third and so on all the way to the forty-seventh. Finally, the building caves in from the bottom. What does it mean? To understand my chilling conclusions, first consider CNN's outline of the events that day and my own simultaneous actions.

September 11: Chronology of Terror
(Adapted from CNN.com US 9/12/2001)

8:45 A.M.: (all times are Eastern Standard Time) A hijacked passenger jet, American Airlines Flight 11 out of Boston, Massachusetts, crashes into the north tower of the World Trade Center, tearing a gaping hole in the building and setting it afire. I am just leaving my house, headed to the CME for the opening of the markets.

9:03 A.M.: A second hijacked airliner, United Airlines Flight 175 from Boston, crashes into the south tower of the World Trade Center and explodes. Both buildings are now burning. Globex electronic trading is shut down. The CME announces it will not open for trading and is evacuating the building. I arrive at the CME just as they order all the markets closed. Panic is starting to spread across the country.

9:17 A.M.: The Federal Aviation Administration shuts down all New York area airports. I start making calls to my customers to inform them that the markets will probably not open and to share information I'm hearing from the CME and my own sources.

9:21 A.M.: The Port Authority of New York and New Jersey orders all bridges and tunnels in the New York area closed.

9:30 A.M.: President Bush, speaking in Sarasota, Florida, says the country has suffered an "apparent terrorist attack."

9:40 A.M.: The FAA halts all flight operations at U.S. airports, the first time in U.S. history that air traffic nationwide has ever been halted.

9:43 A.M.: American Airlines Flight 77 crashes into the Pentagon, sending up a huge plume of smoke. Evacuation begins immediately.

9:45 A.M.: The White House evacuates.

9:57 A.M.: Bush departs Florida. I evacuate the CME building where my offices are under the orders of the Exchange and I head out to meet with a colleague, John Geldermann.

10:05 A.M.: The south tower of the World Trade Center collapses, plummeting into the streets below. A massive cloud of dust and debris forms, slowly drifting away from the building. The whole country is in a state of shock.

10:08 A.M.: Secret Service agents armed with automatic weapons are deployed into Lafayette Park across from the White House.

10:10 A.M.: A portion of the Pentagon collapses.

10:10 A.M.: United Airlines Flight 93, also hijacked, crashes in Somerset County, Pennsylvania, southeast of Pittsburgh.

10:28 A.M.: The World Trade Center's north tower collapses from the top down, peeling apart while releasing a second massive cloud of dust and debris.

10:48 A.M.: Police confirm the crash in Pennsylvania.

1:04 P.M.: Bush, speaking from Barksdale Air Force Base in Louisiana, says that all appropriate security measures are being taken, including putting the U.S. military on high alert worldwide. He asks for prayers for those killed or wounded in the attacks and says, "Make no mistake, the United States will hunt down and punish those responsible for these cowardly acts." By now I am home, calling my family and listening to the President speak.

1:27 P.M.: A state of emergency is declared by the city of Washington, D.C.

1:44 P.M.: The Pentagon says five warships and two aircraft carriers will leave the U.S. Naval Air Station in Norfolk, Virginia, to protect the eastern seaboard from further attack and reduce the number of U.S. warships in port. Two carriers, the USS George Washington and the USS John F. Kennedy, sail for New York. The other ships headed to sea are frigates and guided missile destroyers capable of shooting down aircraft. We are now wondering if the U.S. is at war and with whom.

4:10 P.M.: Forty-seven story Building #7 of the World Trade Center is reported on fire.

5:20 P.M.: Building #7 becomes the third structure at the World Trade Complex to collapse. Evacuated earlier in the day, it was damaged when the twin towers across the street went down hours before. Other nearby buildings are still ablaze.

6:00 P.M.: At 2:30 A.M. local time - hours after the terrorist attacks which targeted financial and military centers in the United States - explosions are heard in Kabul, Afghanistan. It is here that Osama bin Laden, who American officials call the mastermind behind 9/11, is located. Even so, the United States denies any involvement in the explosions. Instead, the attack is credited to the Northern Alliance, a group fighting the Taliban in Afghanistan's ongoing civil war. On hearing the news, I realize how tragic it is that my colleagues Jim and Joe Ritchie, avid supporters of the Afghan people, along with freedom fighter Abdul Haq, have been unable to unite the Northern and Southern tribal chiefs to fight against bin Laden and the Taliban. If they had, perhaps thousands of Americans would have been spared - or not.

Why do I say this? Because maybe just maybe there was more at stake than ideology. Consider -

What lies BENEATH the World Trade Center? I am beginning to wonder what's happened to the investigative reporters working for newspapers and television whose job it is to question everything. Is Chicago's Walter Jacobson the only one left in the country? So many questions from 9/11 remain unanswered and ignored. There is incorrect and partial information on critical issues being distributed to the people of the United States and it's getting worse. Sometimes, the less said is better, but eventually the truth needs to be told.

Remember how many different kinds of police, FBI, and even Secret Service agents were present at Ground Zero? Terrorist investigation aside, what was so valuable that so many had to watch over the site? Could it be those underground vaults in the basement of the World Trade Center?

The New York Mercantile Exchange's COMEX division stored all its deliverable gold and silver there. According to the rumor mill, between two hundred million and one hundred sixty billion dollars in gold bullion was sitting in those underground vaults. Either way it's a lot of money. Could that be why a veritable army of Secret Service and FBI agents with shotguns and automatic weapons stood guard even though all that wealth was in vaults trapped beneath tons of twisted steel and rubble from the collapsed towers?

Ultimately, it took an army of firemen, police officers, and Ground Zero workers to clear those vaults out and load the contents into a convoy of armored Brinks trucks. And it was no easy job. According to the grapevine and the New York Daily News, the COMEX Metals trading division of the NYME kept approximately 3800 gold bars weighing 12 tons on site. How much was it worth? In 2001 prices (the time of the WTC attack), gold was valued at $280/ounce and silver at $4.25/ounce. This means the COMEX gold was worth $100 million dollars. And that's not all. The vault also held about 800,000 ounces of gold that COMEX was storing for other people plus, an additional 102 million ounces of silver. This gold was valued at $200 million while the silver was valued at $430 million. You do the math.

The Toronto Bank of Nova Scotia did, claiming its vault #4 at WTC held $200 million (US) in gold and silver. That adds up, but some other things don't. For instance, a ten- wheel lorry was found in a tunnel under #4 WTC, fully loaded with gold bullion and ready to be moved. Several crushed cars were also found at this lower level. Was someone warned of the eminent collapse of the south tower, someone who loaded the gold and was ready to spirit it away? Normally you can show up anytime with your vault receipts to pick up your gold without notification. But so much that you needed a ten wheeler? (Consider, at the CBOT you just pulled up and loaded or unloaded your car or small truck.)

I ask because I know something about this moving process. I worked for Dr. Jarecki of Mocatta Metals, and had to deal with the huge amounts of gold and silver they hedged. I learned that gold was in deliverable specifications of one hundred ounce bars. This made it easy to deliver against a commodity futures position at the COMEX Exchange. To make these deliveries, the gold or silver had to come from, go to, and be stored in an approved vault. The approved vault for NYMEX/COMEX was beneath the World Trade Center. Curious, how Mocatta had fared, I called a friend there a few days after 9/11. He informed me that they'd had approximately 12 tons of gold and silver in that vault ready for delivery at the exchange. Luckily, they didn't lose it all.

An article I read said $230 million worth of gold and silver had been recovered from Scotia Mocatta and relocated. Subsequently, the metals were still available to guarantee delivery of future contracts traded at the COMEX metal division of the NYMEX. Just between you and me, I figure they had a hard time recovering the silver. Experts say it would take fifty tractor trailers to transport the 30,000, one thousand ounce silver bars because each one is the size of a large commercial brick. I know this because I used to watch the guards load and unload deliverable silver at the Chicago Board of Trade. But there's something more important to consider and it's the only silver lining in the 9/11 cloud, the entire WTC warehouse staff GOT OUT OF THE VAULT SAFELY!

Now that's the good news. The bad news is that there are still holes, and I don't mean in the ground at the World Trade Center. Many people, including me, wonder if the vaults had anything to do with the 9/11 tragedy. Maybe, maybe not. All I can tell you is that the FBI investigation into the matter was linked to the Gold Anti-Trust Action Committee lawsuit which threatened to expose international gold laundering activities including those of the Barrick Gold Corporation.

An industry leader with interests in twenty-five operating mines, Barrick was identified as a middleman laundering gold for the Marcos family of the Philippines and - through certain German banks - for several former Communist states. When I learned this, I thought how things always come full circle. When I worked at Cargill Investor Services, I didn't want the Marcos, the high ranking Viet Cong or the high ranking Chinese army group to open an account with us and they didn't. Once again I was glad I'd gone with my instincts.

And my instincts tell me there are still plenty of mysteries around the WTC vault. Like how much gold was really buried there? Where did it all go? What about that ten-wheeler truck that was fully loaded, ready to depart but didn't get out in time? And how about the importance of the six hundred ton a day global bullion market (of which the buried gold is approximately 2%) and the commodity trading industry to a functioning world? Of course none of this is as crucial as the human side of the 9/11 story.

Cantor Fitzgerald occupied the top floors of the World Trade Center's north tower. Over seven hundred bond traders worked there including, on that fatal day, a young Chicago woman on a business trip. One month earlier, Cantor Fitzgerald had promoted her to the position of CME member and she was leasing her membership from my friend and former boss, John Geldermann. While I didn't know her personally, I'm sure she was thrilled and proud to be a member. I'm positive she wanted it as badly as I did when I was her age. Doubtless, she'd studied, working hard to reach this career threshold. She could've walked in my shoes. Instead, she walked into the north tower that morning. Maybe she looked out the window and saw American Airlines Flight #11 bearing down. Hopefully, someone held her hand in that last moment, as all around her, traders perished in the attack, dying in horrible fashion.

I remember my urgent call to Mr. Geldermann that morning, begging him to get out of the CME. "We have to evacuate," I insisted, "this building is too dangerous." He wanted to stay and pay bills, but I forced him to leave, bribing him with breakfast. As we exited, the streets were full of people milling around, trying to figure out where to go. Everyone was quiet, depressed, and confused. Like the walking dead, they just stared into the empty space before them. It was one of those times when the sound of silence made you scared and uneasy. Nobody joked around - unusual for this crowd - but there was nothing to laugh at. John and I had an almost silent meal. Then we both headed to our respective homes to follow the news and try to understand what was happening to our country.

When I look back, my feelings that day are still a blur, but one thing was crystal clear - life as we knew it would never be the same. My nephew, who was driving into the CME from his home in the suburbs, received a call from his out-trade clerk informing him that trading had been suspended and not to come in. Stunned, Wally made a U-turn and sped home in a fog, anxious to get back to his beautiful, pregnant wife Michelle and hold her close. I'm sure, clerks everywhere made similar calls, but I feel for the clerks in New York - those that survived - because they were the bearers of much worse news.

I can't even imagine the fear filled emotions those individuals experienced along with all New Yorkers and every American across the country, seeing those burning towers and the airliners, inhaling the acrid smoke and the stench of death. A trader friend at a large investment bank across the street from Ground Zero told me he will never forget what he saw and felt that day - people holding hands, jumping from the WTC inferno to their certain deaths below. To this day the image haunts him, torturing him so much that he had to leave his job.

Like my friend, we all left our sense of security behind that day. But what did we gain? A chance to support each other, a new vision of ourselves and our country, and an opportunity to reinvent who we want to be. And now we also know what lies beneath the World Trade Center.

Could that be what caused it all?

Chapter Twenty-Six

POLITICS

March 6, 2001. It's a gorgeous sunny day in Chicago and I'm up early choosing an outfit for work. President George W. Bush is making an appearance at the Chicago Mercantile Exchange today and he's going to give a short speech on the floor. It's 8:00 A.M and I'm ready to leave when the phone rings. John Geldermann, former CME Chairman is calling to say he's near my house on his way to the exchange and can he give me a ride to the Merc. Perfect. By car, it's exactly seven minutes from my door to the CME. I like to be on the floor by 8:30 A.M. for the opening of the S&P, even though cattle and hogs don't open until 9:00, and grains at 9:30. This early start gives me a chance to check my customers' positions and begin making calls.

There's always good security at the exchanges but today the enforcement is especially strict. Members and employees wanting to step on the floor must slide their identification card on the turnstile. The turnstile is similar to those at subways and train stations. Your card unlocks it and it spins around, permitting one person at a time to enter. Then you walk to the x-ray machine and place your briefcase or purse on the conveyor belt. It's like going on a trip everyday and I am - a fast, wild trip to the market.

This morning there's an extra security check because of President Bush. We have to walk through a special, metal detector arch then get wanded by a guard on the other side. Two Secret Service agents are stationed nearby, watching me approach. As I walk through the arch, of course, I set off the alarms. The two agents start laughing. Winking, I say, "You're right. I have on my French, all lace, uplift underwire bra." The minute the guard puts his wand near my chest, the thing starts beeping, the agents blush, and they wave me through the door.

At 10:00 A.M. we're waiting eagerly for the President though he isn't due for several hours. I'm in the break room with my coffee group when I see a young man walk past. He's wearing a long suede coat with a big collar and a large split up the back. It's a duster, the kind of coat cowboys wear while riding their horses through heavy rain or snow. Definitely, not the norm for a pretty, sunny day in Chicago. Hmmm. As he steps forward, the split opens up and I see a large gun hidden beneath. It looks like a sawed off shotgun or a fat gun with a wide nozzle. Shocked, I turn to my group. "Look at that guy," I insist, "he has a large rifle or shotgun under his coat." As he took another step, everyone looked and my friends could clearly see the gun through the split. We figured he must be a Secret Service agent and instinctively, I knew we were right. I could tell by the way he moved and assessed his surroundings. I would even venture to say this agent was part of the Washington D.C. presidential advance team. How did I know? I'd had four wonderful years observing this type of man (Denny!) and I trusted my instincts. Re-assured, my group and I went back to laughing, talking, and watching the market.

Coffee break over, I returned to my trading desk. Right above my head on the catwalk between the electronic boards is the guy in the duster. President Bush isn't expected for another five hours, so I figure Agent Duster is there to protect me and my sexy French bra. Needless to say I felt safe with such a big gun above me, then, since it was a busy day, I put it out of my mind, although occasionally I saw Agent Duster peer out from between the quote boards. The more he peeked, the more it began to bother me. I started thinking maybe he's not an agent at all, but some weird psycho murderer or a hit man waiting to shoot the president. But certainly security would've caught such a person.

Repeating this to myself, I went back to the reality of trading and the excitement on the floor.

It's now two o'clock, the busiest part of the trading day because it's near market close. President Bush arrives and spends thirty minutes in the large S&P pit. He's walking around talking, shaking hands, and signing cards for all the clerks and member traders. By the time he exits the pit, things are getting very loud with a lot of pushing and shoving. It is then that I notice the pit has entered a "fast market." "Fast market" is a technical term that means the exchange pit reporter can't keep up with the erratic quotes being signaled to him from the pit. By declaring a fast market, the reporter is alerting the public that the market is erratic and the quoted prices may not be in sequential order.

I am truly shocked that Mr. Bush is able to take the fast market noise and heat for so long. Most dignitaries who walk around the floor and enter the pit barely last ten minutes, let alone the thirty President Bush has endured. As he exits the pit, he walks directly to a dressing area the Secret Service has roped off and disappears inside. I think he had to change out of his soaking wet shirt before continuing his tour, because he's gone ten minutes. Then Mr. Bush comes out and casually saunters to the cattle area where a small podium and microphone are set up in the pit - right in front of my trading desk. Talk about location!

All the directors and officers of the CME walk up to the podium to give the welcome and introductory speeches. Then President Bush thanks everyone and begins talking about free enterprise and how important our profession is to that concept. He says we are one of the few, major, flourishing examples of free enterprise left in the world. Floor traders, he continues, are the last bastion of unhindered small business. Applauding wildly, the CME members scream their approval. Even though it's not closed, people move away from the S&P pit to get close to the President and hear him speak. I am mesmerized because I believe he's right. The commodity exchanges have certainly given me and many others the opportunity to build our own successful, small businesses, and they provide a path for others to do the same. As I continue to listen, I can't believe how impressed I am with Mr. Bush's speech and the way he's conducted his visit. He's impressed and inspired all the members like me, who had the chance to meet him. He even takes the time to shake our hands, making us each feel like we're the only person in the room. When he gets to me, he smiles and looks at my member badge. I know what he's thinking - a woman in a man's world. I smile back and say, "Nice to meet you Mr. President."

As he walks away, I think about how President Bush's CME visit is different from his predecessors. Maybe that's why it impressed me so much. You see, President Clinton was at the exchange a few years ago, but he was in a private meeting upstairs. President and Mrs. Carter 's visit was short, as was President Reagan's. Soviet President Mikhail Gorbachev greeted people and shook hands, then he and his wife entered the grain pit for ten minutes and attempted to trade. There have been other presidents, American and foreign, who have visited the CME, but this short list is the group I was privileged to meet.

I was also privileged to meet presidential hopefuls who visited the exchange. During the 2008 political campaign, some CME members sponsored an expensive, fund raising cocktail party for Republican candidate, Senator John McCain. Before the event started. Senator McCain, along with his small entourage, came down onto the newly re-designed CME/CBOT floor. I was standing alone between the corn and wheat pits when to my surprise and delight, Senator McCain, also alone, walked up and said, "Hi Joyce, nice to meet you." Then he shook my hand. It was so unexpected that it threw me for a second, but I managed to return his smile and say hello. Just behind him was my friend, Leo Melamed, escorting Senator Joe Lieberman. Leo leaned over, kissed me on the cheek and said, "Hi, honey." Then Joe Lieberman grasped my hand and said, "Hi, Honey." I think Senator Lieberman must've thought my name was "Honey" because Leo is known to be very reserved and he would never call anyone by a pet name. That's why the endearment meant so much to me. You see, Leo and I have known each other many years. We are old, dear friends who share mutual respect. That's why I felt so honored to work with him and to meet and talk with these powerful men.

As I walked off the floor, headed toward my office, I crossed the CBOT lobby. There, I ran into my girlfriend, Karen Waldman. Karen is a tall, long-haired brunette with a beautiful, rosy complexion and legs up to there. She works in the IT department of one of the large

CBOT proprietary trading companies. I invited her to lunch in the Members Lounge overlooking the main trading floor. I said there was going to be a big McCain fundraiser in the visitor's gallery, just outside the restaurant and she might see him and Joe Lieberman. Though short on time, Karen was very excited and immediately said yes.

We finished lunch and got ready to go. As we walked out the door, the dignitaries arrived and leading the way was John McCain. Smiling, he walked right up to me and said, "Hi, Joyce, nice to see you again." Behind the Senator was my old friend, Harvey Paffenroth from the cattle pit, who for once, restrained himself and didn't call me "Choice Joyce." Instead, Harvey kissed me on each cheek and said, "Long time, no see." I think Harvey was trying to conduct himself in a sophisticated manner because he was one of the hosts of the event. Behind Harvey, I saw Leo Melamed and Joe Lieberman. Again, Leo kissed me on the cheek and Senator Lieberman said, "Hi, Honey, how's it going?"

Karen just stared at me with her jaw on the floor. Finally, she spoke. "Joyce," she exclaimed, "I didn't know you knew John McCain and Joe Lieberman!"

I told her that I didn't exactly know them, I'd just met them down on the floor. I guess with five to ten thousand men walking around and only a few women, it was easy for them to remember my name. I was also in the right place at the right time and in life (like in business – especially the trading business!) timing is everything. But of course, that's not nearly as much fun as saying, "John McCain and Joe Lieberman? Why darling, I've known them forever!"

Chapter Twenty-Seven

IS THIS THE END OR THE BEGINNING?

I was attending a Lyric Opera function at the Lake Geneva Country Club in Lake Geneva, Wisconsin, recently when I ran into my favorite bond broker, John Bollero. I told him I was writing this book and that I had written a part about him. As I began to relate the story, John started laughing and said, "Don't tell me, don't tell me! I want to read it."

Many people say the same thing when I begin to recount their "Chapter." They get all excited and can't wait to read the book. Some are interested in the daily life of a trader in the pits. Others are more curious about the wild parties or who I slept with. Let me answer that last question right now.

At the end of this book is a list entitled "To all the men I loved before who traveled in and out of my door." That door is the gateway to my heart. To find out who I slept with, I guess you'll have to read my next book, "Sex and the CBOT." This book, "Joyce, Queen of the Mountain," is about me and the people I care for. The good, the bad, and the ugly who I met on my journey to the top.

As I stood at the bar, reminiscing with John, he re-confirmed many of my thoughts about those people. Even though they hit big highs in the market and made huge amounts of money, in the end, most of the traders we worked with walked away with nothing. Are you surprised? Don't be. It's the nature of the beast. A lot of my colleagues spent everything they made. Some of them were actually living hand to mouth.

One millionaire trader I know invested a lot of money in a dot.com company. You would've thought he'd made millions. Instead, he lost it all. As I said, timing is

everything. Knowing when to get in and when to get out, whether in trading or in life. That's the difference between winning and losing. Barry Lind understood this.

Back in 1969, he had a party at his home just two blocks away from where I live now. Barry owned a large duplex condominium in a vintage building. The living room was three stories high with an old white stone fireplace that reached from the floor to the carved ceiling. Tall stone arches with windows spanned the south end of the space and through these, you could see the magnificent tall buildings and bright lights of the city.

I told Barry I'd attend the party if the band played my favorite Beatles' song. I walked in the door and instantly, the musicians struck up the tune. They closed with the same number at the end of the evening. Imagine one hundred party guests, Barry, me and everyone up dancing and singing "Obladi, oblada, life goes on---la, la, how the life goes on."

And it's true. That's what I'm thinking about as I sit in the living room of my beautiful residence on Lake Shore Drive. To the east are floor to ceiling windows that span seventy-five feet, giving me a magnificent view of the lake. I am watching a fiery sunrise break the horizon over Lake Michigan. The sun is every shade of red and pink. The water is glistening and alive with sharp, choppy waves rolling onto Oak Street Beach. My home is aglow and serene. There are people out strolling and as the sun rises higher, an orange glow glides slowly down my hallway into my all white bedroom. In this gorgeous setting, I think about my life and the people who have shared it.

John Bollero and I are two of the lucky ones. John has a beautiful wife, Kathy, and some lovely children. He has homes in Lake Geneva and in Palm Beach, Florida, and he earned them. Like me, the man worked his butt off trading to accomplish his goals and he is very grateful. So am I.

"Thank you, CBOT and CME," I say, "thank you for giving me the opportunity to be financially successful and make so many friends who have enriched my life." Then I think about the loneliness of being a woman in a man's world. I think how I will never be one of them and of all the times I laughed and cried through painful days and lonely nights. I sing Willie Nelson's song, "To all the men I loved before who traveled in and out my door."

That door to my heart is still open, open for the people and profession I love. I still own my membership at the Chicago Board of Trade. I could sell it and put the cash to better use, but I can't bring myself to do it. I'm not ready to sever this part of my life, the experience and dreams that have made me who I am.

Terry Cullerton once said, "I remember coming onto the floor when I was a little boy and thought it was exciting, thrilling, and it got in my blood."

It was the same for me. I can't explain what attracted me to the exchange, but even now it makes me feel fearless, free, and full of energy. It is the reason I am, and always will be JOYCE, QUEEN OF THE MOUNTAIN.

TO ALL THE MEN I LOVED BEFORE
WHO TRAVELED IN AND OUT MY DOOR

Michael Forbeck
John J. O'Doherty
William (Billy) O'Connor
Butch McGuire
Jim Behrens
Ric Shanahan
Tim Anderson WIZ
Jeffs Kollar
Terrence (Terry) Cullerton
John T. Geldermann
John (Bud) Frazier
Vince Schreiber
Pat Boyle
Fred (Freddie) Brzozowski
Daniel Amstutz
Uncle Julius Frankel
Charlie Di Francesca
Charlie Clement
Everette Klipp
Edmund O'Connor
Michelle Billings

GLOSSARY OF TRADING TERMS

Account Executive – The agent of a commission house who serves customers/traders by entering their commodity futures and options orders, reporting trade executions, advising on trading strategies, etc.

Arbitrage – The simultaneous purchase of cash, futures, or options in one market against the sale of cash, futures or options in a different market in order to profit from a price disparity.

Ask price – An "offer." It indicates a willingness to sell a futures or options on futures contract at a given price.

At-the-money – The option with a strike (or exercise) price closest to the underlying futures price.

Bar chart – A graph of prices, volume and open interest for a specified time period used by the chartist to forecast market trends. For example, a daily bar chart plots each trading session's open, high, low and settlement prices.

Barrel – A unit of volume measure used for petroleum and refined products. 1 barrel = 42 U.S. gallons.

Bear – One who believes prices will move lower.

Bear market – A market in which prices are declining.

Bid price – An offer to buy a specific quantity of a commodity at a stated price or the price that the market participants are willing to pay.

Bid/ask spread – The price difference between the bid and offer price.

Block trade - A privately negotiated futures transaction executed apart from public auction market, either on or off the exchange trading floor. There are minimum order size requirements that vary according to product and order type. Block Trades can only be negotiated with futures, options on futures, and CBOT swap trades.

Bond - Instrument traded on the cash market representing a debt a government entity or of a company.

Brokerage - The fee paid to a broker for executing orders. May be a flat amount or a percentage; also referred to as a commission.

Brokerage house - A firm that handles orders to buy and sell futures and options contracts for customers.

Bull- One who expects prices to rise.

Bull market - A market in which prices are rising.

Buyer's Market - A condition of the market in which there is an abundance of goods available and hence buyers can afford to be selective and may be able to buy at less than the price that previously prevailed. See seller's market.

Call option - A contract between a buyer and seller in which the buyer pays a premium and acquires the right, but not the obligation, to purchase a specified futures contract at the strike price on or prior to expiration. The seller receives a premium and is obligated to deliver, or sell, the futures contract at the specified strike price should a buyer elect to exercise the option. Also see American Style Option and European Style Option.

Cash market - A place where people buy and sell the actual commodities, i.e., grain elevator, bank, etc. Spot usually refers to a cash market price for a physical commodity that is available for immediate delivery. A forward contract is a cash contract in which a seller agrees to deliver a specific cash commodity to a buyer sometime in the future.

Cash price - Current market price of the actual or physical commodity. Also called the spot price.

Central Bank - A government bank that regulates a country's banks and manages a nation's monetary policy. The Federal Reserve is the central bank in the United States,

whereas the European Central Bank (ECB) is the central bank of the European Monetary Union.

Chicago Board of Trade - (CBOT)-Acronym for the Board of Trade of the City of Chicago, Inc. On July 9, 2007, the Chicago Mercantile Exchange Holdings Inc. and **Chicago Board of Trade Holdings, Inc. -** completed the merger of their companies, creating the world's largest and most diverse exchange, CME Group.

Chicago Mercantile Exchange - (CME)-Acronym for the CHICAGO MERCANTILE EXCHANGE INC. On July 9, 2007, Chicago Mercantile Exchange Holdings Inc. and Chicago Board of Trade Holdings, Inc. completed the merger of their companies, creating the world's largest and most diverse exchange now known as CME Group A

Clearing - The procedure through which CME Clearing House becomes the buyer to each seller of a futures contract, and the seller to each buyer, and assumes responsibility for protecting buyers and sellers from financial loss by ensuring buyer and seller performance on each contract.

Clearing firm - A firm approved to clear trades through CME Clearing House. Memberships in clearing organizations are usually held by companies. Clearing members are responsible for the financial commitments of customers that clear through their firm.

Clearing house - An agency or separate corporation of a futures exchange that is responsible for settling trading accounts, collecting and maintaining margin monies, regulating delivery and reporting trade data. CME Clearing is the clearing house for CME.

Clerk - A member's bona fide employee who has been registered by the exchange to work on the trading floor.

Close - The period at the end of the trading session officially designated by the exchange during which all transactions are considered "made at the close." Sometimes used to refer to the closing range.

Closing bell - Any signal which indicates the conclusion of normal daily trading hours in any commodity.

Closing price - The last price of a contract at the end of a trading session.

CME clearing house - The division of CME Group that confirms, clears and settles all CME Group trades. CME Clearing also collects and maintains performance bond funds, regulates delivery and reports trading data.

CME Globex - The first global electronic trading system for futures and options has evolved to become the world's premier marketplace for derivatives trading. With continual enhancements, the platform has effectively enabled CME, already known for innovation, to transform itself into a leading high-tech, global financial derivatives exchange.

CME Group - A combined entity formed by the 2007 merger of the Chicago Mercantile Exchange (CME) and the Chicago Board of Trade (CBOT). We provide the widest range of benchmark futures and options products available on any exchange.

Commission – The one time fee charged by a broker to a customer when the customer executes a futures or option on futures trade through the brokerage firm.

Commodity – In reference to futures trading, the underlying instrument upon which a futures contract is based.

Commodity Futures Trading commission – (CFTC)-Acronym for the Commodity Futures Trading Commission as created by the

Commodity Futures Trading Commission Act of 1974. This government agency regulates the nation's commodity futures industry.

Commodity pool - An enterprise in which funds contributed by a number of persons are combined for the purpose of trading futures contracts or commodity options.

Consumer Price Index - (CPI)-A measuring the average price of consumer goods and services purchased by U.S. households. It is one of several price indices calculated by national statistical agencies. The percent change in the CPI is a measure of inflation. The CPI can be used to index (i.e., adjust for the effects of inflation) wages, salaries, pensions, or regulated or contracted prices.

Contract - An agreement to buy or sell an exchange specified amount of a particular commodity or financial instrument at a specified price. Also, a term of reference describing a unit of trading for a commodity future, as in "5 Lean Hog contracts".

Crude Oil - A mixture of hydrocarbons that exists as a liquid in natural underground reservoirs and remains liquid at atmospheric pressure after passing through surface separating facilities. Crude is the raw material which is refined into gasoline, heating oil, jet fuel, propane, petrochemicals, and other products.

Crush spread - In the soybean futures market, the simultaneous purchase of soybean futures and the sale of soybean meal and soybean oil futures to establish a processing margin.

Current yield - A term used frequently in bond transactions. Current yield is computed by dividing the annual amount of interest by the price paid for the bond or security. If the security is purchased at a discount from the par or principal value, the current yield with be higher than the stated interest or coupon rate.

Daily trading limits - The maximum price range permitted a contract during one trading session. Trading limits are set by the exchange for certain contracts.

Day trading - Establishing a position or multiple positions and then offsetting them within the same day, ending the day with no established position in the market.

Delivery - The term has distinct meaning when used in connection with futures contracts. Delivery generally refers to the changing of ownership or control of a commodity under specific terms and procedures established by the exchange which the contract is traded.

Derivative - A financial instrument whose value is based upon other financial instruments, such as a stock index, interest rates or commodity indexes.

Discount rate - The interest rate that an eligible depository institution is charged to borrow short-term funds directly from a Federal Reserve Bank

Discretionary account - An arrangement by which the holder of the account gives written power of attorney to another person, often his broker, to make trading decisions. Also known as a controlled or managed account.

Equity - (1) Instrument traded on the cash market representing a share in the capital of a company; (2) The net value of a commodity account as determined by combining the ledger balance with an unrealized gain or loss in open positions as marked to the market.

Eurodollars - U.S. dollars on deposit with a bank outside of the United States and, consequently, outside the jurisdiction of the United States. The bank could be either a foreign bank or a subsidiary of a U.S. bank.

Exchange - A central marketplace with established rules and regulations where buyers and sellers meet to trade futures and options on futures contracts. See futures Exchange.

Exchange-for-Physical - (EFP) exchange cash commodity for futures commodity.

Federal funds - In the United States, federal funds are bank reserves at the Federal Reserve. Banks keep reserves at Federal Reserve Banks to meet their reserve requirements and to clear financial transactions. Transactions in the federal funds market enable depository institutions with reserve balances in excess of reserve requirements to lend reserves to institutions with reserve deficiencies. These loans are usually made for 1 day only, i.e. "overnight." The interest rate at which the funds are lent is called the federal funds rate.

Federal funds rate - The rate of interest charged for the use of federal funds.

Federal Reserve System - (Fed)-The central banking system of the United States. Created in 1913 by the enactment of the Federal Reserve Act, it is a quasi-public (part private, part government) banking system composed of (1) the presidentially-appointed Board of Governors of the Federal Reserve System in Washington, D.C.; (2) the Federal Open Market Committee; (3) 12 regional Federal Reserve Banks located in major cities throughout the nation acting as fiscal agents for the U.S. Treasury. The current Federal Reserve Chairman is Dr. Ben S. Bernanke.

Fill-or-kill - order (FOK)-FOK orders are canceled if not immediately filled for the total quantity at the specified price or better.

Flat - Market slang to indicate that all open positions have been offset and an account has no exposure to market risk. Three common positions in the market are long, short or flat.

Floor broker ñ A professional who is registered with the CFTC to execute orders on the floor of an exchange for the account of another. They receive a fee for doing this.

Floor trader - An individual who is registered with the CFTC to execute trades on the floor of an exchange for his own account. Also referred to as a local.

Fundamental analysis - The study of supply and demand information.

Futures commission merchant - (FCM)-An individual or organization which solicits or accepts orders to buy or sell futures or options contracts and accepts money or other assets from customers in connection with such orders. Each FCM must be registered with the Commodity Futures Trading Commission.

Futures contract - A legally binding agreement to buy or sell a commodity or financial instrument at a later date. Futures contracts are standardized according to the quality, quantity and delivery time and location for each commodity.

Futures exchange -A board of trade designated by the Commodity Futures Trading Commission to trade futures or option contracts on a particular commodity.

Futures Industry Association - (FIA)-Futures Industry Association. A national not-for-profit futures industry trade association that represents the brokerage community on industry, regulatory, political, and educational issues.

GALAX-C - CME hand-held trading terminals.

Hedger - An individual or firm who uses the futures market to offset price risk when intending to sell or buy the actual commodity. See pure hedger, selective hedger.

Hedging - (1) Taking a position in a futures market opposite to a position held in the cash market to minimize the risk of financial loss from an adverse price change; (2) A purchase or sale of futures as a temporary substitute for a cash transaction which will occur later. See long hedge and short hedge.

High - The highest price of the day for a particular futures contract.

House – (1) A designation that refers to proprietary, non-segregated clearing member firm trading activity; (2) A clearing member or a firm.

House account – Clearing firm's proprietary, non-segregated trading account.

Introducing broker – (IB)-A firm or person engaged in soliciting or accepting and handling orders for the purchase or sale of futures contracts, subject to the rules of a futures exchange, but not in accepting any money or securities to margin any resulting trades or contracts. The IB is associated with a correspondent futures commission merchant and must be licensed by the CFTC.

Inverted market – A futures market in which the relationship between two delivery months of the same commodity is abnormal.

Leading indicators – Market indicators that signal the state of the economy for the coming months. Some of the leading indicators include: average manufacturing workweek, initial claims for unemployment insurance, orders for consumer goods and material, percentage of companies reporting slower deliveries, change in manufacturers' unfilled orders for durable goods, plant and equipment orders, new building permits, index of consumer expectations, change in material prices, prices of stocks, change in money supply.

Lead month –The futures contract trading in lead month position on the trading floor or electronically; the most current contract month in which delivery may take place, closest to the current point in time.

Leg – Each component transaction of a spread or swap.

Light Crude – Crude oil with a low specific gravity and high API gravity due to the presence of a high proportion of light hydrocarbon fractions.

Limit – See Price Limit.

Limit order – A Limit order allows the buyer to define the maximum price to pay and the seller the minimum price to accept (the limit price). A Limit order remains on the book until the order is either executed, canceled or expires. Any portion of the order that can be matched is immediately executed.

Liquidate – To offset an existing position.

Liquidity – A condition that describes the ability to execute orders of any size quickly and efficiently without a substantial affect on the price.

Locals – Exchange members who trade for their own accounts and/or fill orders.

London Inter-bank Offered Rate – (LIBOR)-The price at which short term deposits are traded among major banks in London. Basically, the interest rate that banks charge each other for loans (usually in Eurodollars). The LIBOR is officially fixed once a day by a small group of large London banks, but the rate changes throughout the day.

Long – One who has bought futures or options contracts to create an open position or owns a cash commodity. Opposite of Short.

Long hedge – The purchase of a futures contract in anticipation of an actual purchase in the cash commodity market. Used by processors or exporters as protection against an advance in the cash price. See hedge.

Lot – A unit of trading (used to describe a designated number of contracts). For example, a trade quantity of one equals a "one lot;" a trade quantity of four equals a "four lot." Also called cars.

Low – The lowest price of the day for a particular futures contract.

Maintenance margin – maintenance performance bond .The minimum equity that must be maintained for each contract in a customer's account subsequent to deposit of the initial performance bond. If the equity drops below this level, a deposit must be made to bring the account back to the initial performance bond level.

Managed account - An arrangement by which the owner of the account gives written power of attorney to someone else, usually the broker or a commodity trading advisor, to buy and sell without prior approval of the account owner. Often referred to as a discretionary Account.

Managed futures - The term managed futures describes an industry comprised of professional money managers kown as commodity trading advisors (CTAs). These trading advisors manage client assets on a discretionary basis using global futures markets as an investment medium. Trading advisors take positions based on expected profit potential. All CTAs involved must be registered with the Commodity Futures Trading Commission (CFTC), a US government regulatory agency.

Margin - See Performance Bond.

Margin call - See Performance Bond Call.

Market-if-touched - (MIT)-An order that automatically becomes a market order if the price is reached. An MIT order to buy becomes a limit order if and when the instrument trades at a specific or lower trigger price; an MIT order to sell becomes a limit order if and when the instrument trades at a specified or higher trigger price.

Market maker - A firm or person with trading privileges on an exchange who has an obligation to buy when there is an excess of sell orders and to sell when there is an excess of buy orders. In the futures industry, this term is sometimes loosely used to refer to a floor trader or local who, in speculating for his own account, provides a market for commercial users of the market.

Market-on-close - (MOC)-An order submitted at any time within a trading session, but only executed on the close.

Market order - (MKT)-An order placed at any time during the trading session to immediately execute the entire order at the best available offer price (for buy orders) or bid price (for sell orders).

Market reporter - A person employed by the exchange and located in or near the trading pit who records prices as they occur during trading.

Member – An individual admitted to membership on the exchange or any of its Divisions.

Membership or membership interest-The trading right associated with a Class B Share in any of the following classes: Class B-1 (CME Membership), Class B-2 (IMM Membership), Class B-3 (IOM Membership) and Class B-4 (GEM Membership).

Minimum price fluctuation - The smallest increment of price movement possible in trading a given contract often referred to as a tick. The minimum unit by which the price of a commodity can fluctuate, as established by the Exchange.

Money supply - The amount of money in the economy, consisting primarily of currency in circulation plus deposits in banks: M-1 U.S. money supply consisting of currency held by the public, traveler's checks, checking account funds, NOW and super- NOW accounts, automatic transfer service accounts, and balances in credit unions. M-2 U.S. money supply consisting M-1 plus savings and small time deposits (less than $100,000) at depository institutions, overnight repurchase agreements at commercial banks, and money market mutual fund accounts. M-3 U.S. money supply consisting of M-2 plus large time deposits ($100,000 or more) at depository institutions, repurchase agreements with maturities longer than one day at commercial banks, and institutional money market accounts.

National Futures Association - (NFA)-The self regulatory organization of the futures industry. Chartered by Congress in 1981, the NFA regulates the activities of its member brokerage firms and their employees. Overseen by the Commodity Futures Trading Commission (CFTC).

Net position - The difference between the long contracts and the short contracts held in any one commodity.

Not held - A discretionary note on an order telling the floor broker that he or she won't be held accountable if the trade is executed outside the requirements of the order.

Notice day - The day the buyer with the oldest long position is matched with the seller's intent and both parties are notified of delivery obligations.

Offer - (ask or sell)-An offer to sell a specific quantity of a commodity at a stated price. (Opposite of a bid.)

Opening - The period at the beginning of the trading session officially designated by the exchange during which all transactions are considered made "at the opening."

Open interest - The total number of futures contracts long or short in a delivery month or market that has been entered into and not yet offset or fulfilled by delivery Also known as **Open Contracts -** or Open Commitments. Each open transaction has a buyer and a seller, but for calculation of open interest, only one side of the contract is counted.

Open order - An order that remains good until filled, canceled, or eliminated

Open outcry - A method of public auction for making bids and offers in the trading pits of futures exchanges.

Order-cancels - order (OCO)-An order qualifer that consists of two linked orders, typically (but not always) a Limit order and a Stop order, that both work until one order is filled, at which time the other order is canceled.

Out of-the-money - A term used to describe an option that has no intrinsic value. A call option with a strike price higher or lower than the current market value.

Over the Counter - (OTC) Market-A market in which custom-tailored contracts such as stocks and foreign currencies are bought and sold between counterparties and are not exchange traded.

Pit - The area on the trading floor where trading in a specific futures or options contracts is conducted by open outcry.

Position - An obligation to perform in the futures or options market. A long position is an obligation to buy at a specified date in the future. A short position is an obligation to sell

Position limit - The maximum number of speculative futures contracts one can hold as determined by the Commodity Futures Trading Commission and/or the exchange.

Position trader - A trader who takes a position in anticipation of a longer term trend in the market.

Price limit - The maximum daily price fluctuations on a futures contract during any one session, as determined by the Exchange. (Also known as limit).

Primary dealer - A designation given by the Federal Reserve System to commercial banks or broker/dealers who meet specific criteria. Among the criteria are capital requirements and meaningful participation in the Treasury auctions.

Prime rate - Interest rate charged by institutional banks to their larger most creditworthy customers.

Producer Price Index - (PPI)-A measure of the average change in prices received by domestic producers for their output. Most of the data is collected through a systematic sampling of producers in manufacturing, mining, and service industries.

Put option - A contract that provides the purchaser the right (but not the obligation) to sell a futures contract at an agreed price (the strike price) at any time during the life of the option. A put option is purchased in the expectation of a decline in price.

Quantity - Number of units or lots of a futures contract. Also called size.

Quote - The price, bid, or asked price of either cash commodities or futures contracts.

Rally - An upward movement of prices. The opposite of a decline.

Range - The difference between the highest and lowest prices recorded during a given trading session.

Resting Order - An order away from the market, waiting to be executed.

Round-turn - A completed transaction involving both a purchase and a liquidating sale.

Runners - Messengers who rush orders taken by phone clerks to brokers in the pit.

Scalp - To trade for small gains. Scalping normally involves establishing and liquidating a position quickly, often within seconds.

Scalper - A speculator on an exchange floor who trades in and out of the market on very small price fluctuations. The scalper, trading in this manner, provides market liquidity.

Seller - A person who takes a short futures position or grants (sells) a commodity option.

Settlement price - The official daily closing price of futures contracts.

Short ñ A futures or options position where you have been a seller. The opposite of long.

Speculator - An individual who accepts market risk in an attempt to profit by correctly anticipating future price movements.

Spot market - The market in which cash transactions for the physical commodity occurs.

Spread - The price difference between two contracts. Holding a long and a short position in two or more related futures or options on futures contracts, with the objective of profiting from a change in the price relationship.

Stock index - A statistic reflecting the composite value of a selected group of stocks.

Stop limit order - A resting Stop Limit order is triggered when the designated price is traded on the market. The order is executed at all price levels between the trigger price and the limit price. If not completed filled order remains in the market.

Swap (OTC) - A custom-tailored, individually negotiated transaction designed to manage financial risk, usually over a period of one to 12 years. The transaction enables each party to manage exposure to commodity prices or index values. Settlements are made in cash.

Swaps-Simultaneous purchase and sale of currencies or interest rate products in spot and forward market transactions.

Treasury Bill - A Treasury bill is a short-term U.S. government obligation with an original maturity of one year or less.

Treasury Bond - Government-debt security with a maturity of more than 10 years.

Treasury Note - Government-debt security with a maturity of one to 10 years.

Volume - The number of contracts in futures or options on futures transacted during a specified period of time.

Yield curve - A chart that graphically depicts the yields of different maturity bonds of the same credit quality and type.